Radical Encouragement
Creating Cultures for Learning

Radical Encouragement
Creating Cultures for Learning

Steve Williams and Rupert Wegerif

Imaginative Minds Ltd
Birmingham
2006

ACKNOWLEDGEMENTS

The authors thank all members of the N-RAIS team for their help in providing information, material and inspiration for this book. We would also like to thank Martin Renton for contributing an account of his experiences of professional development with N-RAIS.

First published 2006 by Imaginative Minds Ltd
Leonard House, 321 Bradford Street, Birmingham B5 6ET

ISBN: 1-904806-03-1

Contents

STEVE WILLIAMS is editor of *Teaching Thinking and Creativity* magazine. He has taught and written widely about Philosophy for Children and thinking skills. He is co-author of *The Philosophy Club: An Adventure in Thinking* and *Talking Pictures: Thinking Through Photographs.*

RUPERT WEGERIF is a Professor of Education at Exeter University. His main research interest is the practice of dialogue in teaching and learning. He is author of *Thinking and Learning with ICT* and *Dialogic Education and Technology.* He is co-author of *Thinking Together.*

Preface

*E*veryone involved in education today faces a difficult and persistent problem: how can education be creative, supportive and motivating while at the same time rigorous, methodical and challenging?

This book describes a project, N-RAIS, that began to tackle this problem using a number of imaginative approaches such as philosophical enquiry, the teaching of thinking skills and coaching.

The title N-RAIS stands for *Northumberland Raising Aspirations in Society*. It is an education and training project that operates in many of the areas of Northumberland where averages for family income, educational achievement and progression to higher education are low – the sorts of areas often described in official reports as 'disadvantaged'. Innovations introduced into schools by N-RAIS consultants have been received enthusiastically by many local teachers, pupils and parents because the project team has demonstrated new possibilities for teaching and learning.

After consultation with the authors, the N-RAIS team adopted the term 'Radical Encouragement' to describe its work and to guide future developments. We believe that any institution wishing to improve the quality and effectiveness of the education it offers would need to adopt strategies that embody many of the principles of Radical Encouragement. That is why the work of the N-RAIS project is important. We hope you will agree. It is certainly a more optimistic and radical approach to raising achievement in a school than trying to attract pupils of higher ability at the expense of other schools in the local community.

Introduction

The N-RAIS story starts in the Berwick region of Northumberland when, in 2000, headteachers of all 22 local schools supported a bid to raise educational aspirations and achievements in the area. The Steering Group was initiated by Bill Humphries and chaired by Elizabeth Bowen, headteacher of Grove Special School. Working with *Northumberland Strategic Partnership,* the group secured £250,000 from the government's Single Regeneration Budget via *One North East*, a regional development agency. Berwick RAIS became Northumberland RAIS (N-RAIS) in 2003, when *One North East* provided funding for expansion following a very positive evaluation of the Berwick project.

The N-RAIS team works in the community, mainly through local schools, and consists of two directors, seven consultants and two administrators. The directors and consultants give free advice, support and training to teachers and work directly with children and young people on special occasions. They also run courses for parents, community groups and some local businesses. At the time of writing, schools in Northumberland are organised into four stages: first schools (age range 4-9), middle schools (age range 9-12) and high schools (age range 12-18).

The long-term aim of the N-RAIS project is: 'to help young people become more intelligent, confident and emotionally balanced in order to recognise, pursue and achieve their potential'. If this can be achieved, then the local area will benefit from a self-strengthening culture of learning and enterprise.

The N-RAIS team adopted a set of approaches, tried successfully in Berwick, that would give an immediate boost to the sorts of dispositions and skills necessary for intelligence, confidence and emotional resilience to flourish. So, for example, team members used strategies to promote dispositions such as curiosity, adventurousness and persistence. At the same time, they helped teachers to help learners develop the skills necessary to handle intellectual challenges common to subjects across the curriculum. The strategies N-RAIS consultants used most frequently were philosophical enquiry, the teaching of thinking skills and coaching (a supportive process of setting goals, trying out, evaluating performance and trying again).

The N-RAIS team usually introduced the strategies to schools by offering a one-day event in which N-RAIS consultants taught a class of students, using each strategy in turn or a combination of all of them. The obvious advantage of such a starting point is that staff were able to see immediately how their pupils responded to new challenges. They were often impressed by what they saw.

Staff were then invited to introduce one of the approaches into their own work with students. N-RAIS consultants offered a variety of starting points to staff. A consultant could work alongside a teacher in the classroom on something they agreed to develop together. Alternatively, a teacher could attend a two-day N-RAIS course on each of the strategies. The important point is that collaboration between N-RAIS staff and each school was carried out through a voluntary process of negotiation rather than compulsion – and the support offered was free.

Schools take up the N-RAIS strategies

As schools in the area began to take up the N-RAIS offers of support and training, after-school courses flourished in the region as never before and a growing number of teachers began to report positive changes in both themselves and their pupils. Even parents began to notice differences in the ways their children talked about lessons at school. The spoken and written comments by parents and teachers that follow express some of this enthusiasm.

Parents' Comments

'We have noticed Martin has a lot more confidence in speaking up, especially when meeting people for the first time. I can't thank you enough for giving Martin a lot more confidence. This group has helped him immensely. He has lost his nervousness and his speech is a lot better. If something comes up in conversation and is related to a topic covered in a philosophy lesson, Martin will ask our views. His questions make us have to think before we can answer.'

'Olivia's reasoning has improved. She is always considering the consequences of certain actions and ideas. Also, her range of vocabulary has improved. She often surprises us with the words she uses.'

'We feel philosophy has been one of the factors that has improved Robyn's confidence. She shares many of her philosophy sessions with us and is always curious about our opinions.'

Teachers' comments

'N-RAIS had a huge effect on my teaching and the way I teach my class. My pupils are better able to learn independently, they ask better questions, they give more complete answers and they talk about learning with their peers. It makes me realise how much more they can learn than I had previously assumed.'

'I found the N-RAIS courses profoundly informative and rewarding. After using some of the strategies I learned, I believe that my pupils' self-esteem has risen, their oracy has improved and their thinking is more critical.'

'Our school has benefited significantly from N-RAIS over the past three years. The strategies have had a very positive impact on standards of teaching and learning. This year we have noticed a big improvement in the oracy of year 5 children who have done philosophy. The quality of their questioning has risen dramatically.'

'Setting my students tasks to develop their thinking skills has livened up my lessons and drawn the students' attention to important concepts such as causes, reasons and categories.'

'Philosophy has helped pupils to disagree without falling out with one another and in this school that's quite an achievement. I've been impressed with the improvement in the quality of their questions and the way they stick with questions and try to think through all the implications.'

Connections between the strategies

Teachers in schools that tried out more than one strategy found that they seemed to overlap and strengthen each other. One school asked N-RAIS staff to help coach children to set up and run a school council. The teachers realised that the philosophical enquiry they had been employing was the perfect preparation for the in-depth discussion required in class and council meetings. The philosophy sessions had also cultivated dispositions such as curiosity, reflectiveness and perseverance that would be essential to the new venture.

In other schools, the process of goal setting, trying out, reviewing and trying again that was distinctive of coaching events transferred back to the classroom to be applied in lessons designed to improve pupils' thinking skills.

What made the strategies effective for teachers and learners? And what connections made them complement each other? It seemed that each strategy strengthened both skills and dispositions. *Philosophy for Children* gave learners the opportunities to develop their curiosity, to fashion good questions, talk collaboratively and learn the basics of critical thinking. *Thinking skills initiatives* gave students practice in essential thinking 'moves', such as comparing and categorising, while also requiring them to display dispositions such as reflectiveness and persistence. Coaching helped learners to be self-encouraging, strategic and imaginative, while also providing them with some useful tactics to keep their attention focused on positive goals. Also, and we feel this is important, the strategies helped learners to change the stories they had developed about themselves as learners into more positive and empowering ones.

Overall, the N-RAIS project involved high levels of encouragement targeted at the development of the kinds of dispositions, skills and self-images that are fundamental for continued learning. For this reason, the N-RAIS team adopted the term 'Radical Encouragement' to give coherence to its work and to provide a guide for the development of new strategies. In the next chapter, we explore the concept of Radical Encouragement in more depth and expand on the complex web of dispositions and skills that are cultivated by the N-RAIS strategies for teaching and learning.

1

Radical Encouragement Explained

Radical Encouragement is an approach to learning in schools and communities through developing dispositions, skills and strategies that lead to success in learning. In this chapter, we outline the rationale for Radical Encouragement, introduce examples of key dispositions and discuss implications for teaching.

ALL SUCCESSFUL ATTEMPTS at enabling people to learn better and expand their horizons depend on effective encouragement. Discouraged students will, all too easily, talk themselves down, imagine their own potential within narrow limits and reign in their aspirations. Discouragement is a virus that attacks those whose constitutions have been weakened by self-defined failures. Teachers are not immune from the virus, particularly when they lack control over what they teach, how they teach and how their teaching will be judged. And, of course, students who are discouraged will often discourage their teachers and parents. So a basic first step in any educational institution should be to accept the sovereign importance of encouragement. The next, more demanding, priority is to work out what to focus encouragement on and how best to do it. If successful, then teachers would not so often say or think the kinds of things listed on the following page.

Discouraged Learners

'One of my pupils has given up on maths. She has lost confidence and says: *I'm just no good at it*.'

'Some of my pupils are too dependent on me. They don't feel they are able to struggle through problems by themselves.'

'I know that one of my pupils loves to sing but she is afraid to perform in case other pupils make fun of her.'

'Some pupils are discouraged because they can't compete in tests. They have labelled themselves as *unintelligent*.'

'Some pupils are so discouraged in school they behave badly in class.'

'Some pupils seem afraid to show an interest in lessons because they fear being identified as *geeks*.'

'Some pupils will only show an interest in things that they feel they are good at.'

'Pupils rarely think aloud because they don't want to risk being wrong.'

'I have tried to make my lessons more intellectually challenging but my pupils preferred the less demanding ones. Now I just teach to the test. It's less risky.'

Encouraging positive dispositions

We must accept that discouraged students who make the sort of comments listed opposite have developed destructive dispositions. We are using the word disposition here to mean a 'tendency to think or behave in certain ways under certain conditions'.[1] So, for example, a person could be adventurous when faced with a physical challenge but timid when faced with an intellectual one. No-one is entirely lacking in positive dispositions. What marks out discouraged students is that they fail to show positive dispositions in many learning contexts that we believe are important for their intellectual, physical, emotional and interpersonal development. Where positive dispositions are lacking negative ones develop, such as dispositions towards anger, frustration, disruption and self-criticism.

Dispositions form the weft and weave of stories we tell to ourselves. Our stories have developed out of our previous experiences and our perceptions of those experiences are shaped by cultures that influence us and the care shown to us by other people. So, for example, an early aptitude for games or an effective short-term memory can lead children, with parental approval, to self-stories like 'I'm good at sport' or 'I'm clever'. On the other hand, contemporary fashions can lead people to reject things they might otherwise find fulfilling, as in: 'writing poetry is for girls'.

So to display positive dispositions in situations where one risks failure or ridicule requires courage, not least because it contradicts deeply embedded self-stories. Therefore, when teachers try to extend positive dispositions into new areas they should be aware that their task is personal and cultural. It is not just a matter of applying new curricula and teaching methods.

What, then, are the kinds of dispositions we should target for our encouragement? There could never be a settled super-list of dispositions. Several renowned educationalists have come up with sensible selections. David Perkins[2], Art Costa[3] and Guy Claxton[4] have all succeeded in compiling coherent lists (Costa calls them 'Habits of Mind'). On the following page, we list 11 key dispositions. Each one has implications for teaching.

Positive Dispositions for Learning

The disposition to be adventurous

The disposition to be careful

The disposition to be curious

The disposition to be dialogical

The disposition to be philosophical

The disposition to be imaginative

The disposition to be reflective

The disposition to be collaborative

The disposition to be strategic

The disposition to be persistent

The disposition to encourage oneself and others

We expand these dispositions on the next page and suggest ways that the main N-RAIS strategies of philosophy, thinking skills and coaching can help to develop them.

Stories and dispositions

Teachers who want their pupils to develop these kinds of dispositions will most likely weave them into stories they tell about the world, the culture and the people around them. They might tell stories about the collaboration of great scientists and musicians. They might reflect on times when they themselves succeeded or failed to collaborate. They will seek out examples of collaboration by pupils in the school and work those into stories. They will ask pupils to tell stories about collaborations. Most importantly, they will hold the door open for students to enter, as characters, stories of collaboration, adventurousness or persistence by displaying appropriate dispositions.

It is often said in educational circles that what isn't assessed isn't taught. It is even truer to say that what isn't made part of a story isn't noticed and certainly isn't taken to heart. The importance of teachers trying to enliven schools with stories involving combinations of positive dispositions cannot be overstated. The greater challenge is to have pupils accept that they can be willing actors in those stories.

The disposition to be adventurous

To be adventurous is to take risks and to push at the limits of one's competence and comfort. A classroom environment that encourages tentative questions and answers is a very positive place for learning. Learners shouldn't fear being wrong. They should be especially encouraged to consider unfamiliar ideas and try out new activities. There is no better activity than philosophical enquiry for enabling an environment that encourages students and teachers to take risks with ideas.

Being adventurous is also important for sustaining another important disposition – persistence. One's appetite for regular practice at a sport or musical instrument will dwindle if one is afraid of competing or performing. Being adventurous involves risking failure, setting goals and not giving up. It means not being put off doing something simply because other people you know do it better than you. An element of coaching (or intensive encouragement), based on knowledge of a person's interests and ambitions, is often essential to fostering willingness to take a risk.

The disposition to be careful

Carefulness complements adventurousness. Students must learn not only to control impulsivity but also to strive for accuracy and precision and understand when these qualities are important.

Discussion with peers is one of the best ways to learn control of impulsivity, particularly when discussion partners take the views of others into account before reaching a conclusion. Learners may need to be shown how to generate alternatives, compare them and make choices supported by reasons. Carefulness also has an interpersonal dimension, suggesting concern for others.

Philosophical enquiry and thinking skills strategies help to develop both care and adventurousness by encouraging pupils to generate ideas and then reflect on them in collaborative discussions. Coaching students in techniques of reviewing after trying something out also helps them to take greater care over their subsequent tasks.

The disposition to be curious

Curiosity is the tendency to wonder, find problems, notice anomalies and formulate questions. It is perhaps the most important of all the intellectual dispositions because it creates intellectual energy. Curiosity develops when teachers require their students to create questions in spoken and written form, welcome questions and use them as the starting points for significant enquiry.

Questioning should be a subject within all other subjects in the curriculum. Learners should be aware of the effects of questions in school and personal life and the differences that re-framing questions can make. For example, there is a world of difference between 'Why aren't I any good at history?' and 'What can I find about this history topic that interests me?' or 'Why isn't my husband any good?' and 'Does my husband value the same things in marriage as I do?'

All the N-RAIS strategies give prominence to questioning. Thinking skills activities, such as those that require students to categorise and compare or rank items of study, will generate a host of important questions such as: 'What are the similarities and differences between these things?' 'What are the most significant issues?' 'In what ways do these categories overlap?' When the activities are over, it is most important for these kinds of questions to be internalised by students so that they have a repertoire of questions to apply to learning situations they face in the future. This is the key to independent learning. Armed with clusters of good questions and encouraged to see questioning as one of humanity's greatest resources, students' own curiosities will be strengthened and developed.

Philosophical enquiry is a strategy that starts and ends with students' questions. It anchors the whole process of questioning and the disposition to be curious in a regular activity. Teachers in schools that take up philosophy often report that this, more than anything else, has helped to make the school a more stimulating place where curiosity thrives.

Coaching, another of the N-RAIS techniques, also requires self-questioning of a profound kind: 'What are my aspirations?' 'Why do I feel confident doing an intellectual activity and not a physical one?' 'How can other people help me?' 'How can I help myself?'

Only a curriculum which promotes curiosity and questioning has any chance of producing independent, adventurous learners.

The disposition to be dialogical

To be dialogical is to be open towards others and towards alternative perspectives. It implies being drawn towards shared enquiry with the aim of learning something with or from others. The disposition to be dialogical is an essential prerequisite of all independent learning because what (and how) we learn *with* others becomes internalised as a resource for our own future thinking. It is likely that the ability to think creatively at all originally comes from internalized dialogue.[5] Seeking dialogue is closely linked with other dispositions, such as curiosity, imagination and collaboration.

Dialogue requires a reciprocal relationship between participants to listen, respond and seek meaning. To nurture dialogical dispositions, teachers create opportunities for enquiry in the classroom about questions that have meanings for students. This will mean a shift from provider of all knowledge to enquiry planner and guide.

The strategies promoted by the N-RAIS project rely on good quality dialogue and the dispositions of teachers and students to be dialogical. Does this mean that if students are not very open towards others and towards alternative perspectives, then philosophical enquiry, teaching thinking and coaching cannot work? No, because these strategies exercise and develop such vital dialogical capacities. Many teachers report that when they start philosophy, they are often surprised by the interesting questions pupils come up with and by the quality of some of the reasoning that follows. It takes a while, however, for children to listen carefully to each other, to accept reasonable criticism and to be open to alternative points of view. Teachers have to work hard to develop procedures and ground rules to help pupils progress. Yet the results make the effort worthwhile. Discussions work better and teachers often report that pupils are more open to dialogue in all areas of school life.

Coaching and thinking skills strategies also contribute to developing the kinds of reciprocal relationships of listening and responding that are so important for the intellectual and emotional development of students. Lessons built around collaborative intellectual or physical challenges will always inevitably both depend on dialogue and foster it. The essential point is we learn to think well by thinking with others, so challenges that lead to dialogues are particularly valuable.

The disposition to be philosophical

To be philosophical is to strive for integrity by developing our own values and attitudes to life through dialogue with ourselves and others. Motivation is also in large part a product of our own personal philosophy – our sense of what, for us, is significant.

Philosophical thinking helps give coherence to the school curriculum because it seeks connections between principles and particulars with questions such as: 'What are the principles of truth and how do they apply in the subjects of literature, history and science?' Philosophical thinking is particularly sensitive to concepts, those essential ideas we use to organise our understanding of the world.

Regular exposure to philosophical enquiry will develop this disposition and the N-RAIS project has made philosophy one of its priorities. In the past, arguments for philosophical enquiry in schools have focused on its benefit to the thinking skills of pupils. It is certainly true that programmes such as *Philosophy for Children* are good vehicles for developing children's skills in reasoning, questioning and identifying inconsistencies and making connections. Yet just as important is the effect philosophical discussion has on a person's willingness to reflect on some of the big concepts and questions of life. People should be able to reflect on what a concept like 'success' means for them. Such reflection implies underlying questions like: 'Should everyone accept the same criteria for success?' or 'Can success for one person be failure for another?'

It is significant that when pupils at a first school in Northumberland were coached to participate in school decision-making, they started by discussing the concept of fairness. What would be a fair way to make decisions? If someone didn't like the decision would that mean it was unfair to them? Without this kind of personal exploration of philosophical issues through dialogue, projects to change behaviour and attitudes in schools will depend on the rhetorical powers of teachers. But a culture of stories (see page 13), when open to philosophical questioning and genuine dialogue between teachers and pupils, provides an ideal context for developing self-sustaining values.

The disposition to be imaginative

To be imaginative is to visualize – to produce and use vivid images. It is to look for connections, employing metaphors, similes and analogies. It is to empathise with the emotions and thoughts of others. Imaginative people are inventive, seeking to combine items which are not ordinarily connected in order to create new meanings. Moreover, an imaginative person is open to new learning and tries to reconcile new experiences with older knowledge.

To be imaginative is to generate alternatives and compare them. Imagination is a driving force of creativity but we must remember that creating is not a structureless process. It depends on abilities, knowledge of traditions and willingness to evaluate work using appropriate and challenging critical criteria.

Remaining open to new learning is particularly important for students in teenage years when their patterns of behaviour, both positive and negative, have been well established. We should never cease from trying to interest learners and encouraging them to re-evaluate their experiences, preferences and opinions. Teaching for imagination means being alert to the developing interests and self-stories of students and giving them a growing amount of independence to follow their interests through substantial pieces of work.

The N-RAIS strategies contribute to the engagement of students' imaginations. In coaching situations, people are often asked to visualize themselves achieving their goals. This regular imagining of powerful images and feelings may be as important as the standard notions of 'willpower' and 'determination' for seeing a task through to the end.

Perhaps imagination is as important as reasoning for good thinking. Imagining alternatives is the starting point of all critical thinking because we use imagination to ask critical questions such as: 'How could things have turned out differently?' 'What arguments weren't considered?' 'What wasn't expressed that should have been?' 'What could have been expressed differently?' 'What might change given the influence of new factors?'

Many of the thinking skills activities promoted by the N-RAIS team encourage pupils to generate alternative possibilities for comparisons, selections and explanations. Pupils are encouraged to consider all of these before rejecting any of them prematurely.

Philosophical enquiry has its own distinctive contribution to make in developing the disposition to be imaginative – when thinking philosophically, one constantly asks questions that begin 'what if' and one is open to a wide range of possible answers.

The disposition to be reflective

To be reflective is to be disposed towards reviewing one's experiences. It means being aware of one's own thoughts, feelings and actions – and their outcomes. Teachers promote reflectiveness when they give their pupils regular opportunities to discuss aspects of their thinking and learning such as:

- the strategies they used for a particular task
- the dispositions they felt were needed in the given context
- the difficulties they encountered and how they tried to overcome those difficulties
- the ways they were influenced by others while working together

All this is best done through dialogue. The use of worksheets with repetitive prompts such as: 'What did you find hard/easy?' is a poor substitute. Dialogues about learning will inevitably be shaped by the nature of each specific task and the students' particular responses to it.

Philosophy for Children, coaching and teaching thinking are all reflective activities and can provide models for reflection in other areas of the curriculum. Coaching is, to a large extent, based on the process of setting goals and reviewing performance. Teaching thinking relies on having pupils reflect on how they handled a concept or tackled a problem and then seeing connections with other problems and concepts. Philosophical enquiry is a reflective process in its own right and, once established, lends itself to use by teachers and pupils across the curriculum whenever there is some deep thinking to be done.

The disposition to be collaborative

There are many ways to collaborate. To have a disposition to collaborate is to *seek out* appropriate opportunities to work with others. Sometimes working on one's own is best but unless one has learned how to collaborate in a wide range of situations, one will never be able to evaluate the benefits and drawbacks of joint work or realise the ways that individual work feeds into effective collaboration and vice versa.

Collaboration is also an essential vehicle for developing other key dispositions and is a prerequisite for the kind of reciprocal encouragement among peers that is so positive and powerful. The N-RAIS strategies stimulate collaborative work and collaborative dispositions. They provide good models of how to orchestrate collaborative learning in all kinds of projects and lessons. Their lasting value, however, comes from the fact that they not only foster and exercise collaboration, they enable people to reflect on the quality of their collaborations. Thus, they come to understand how the nature of collaboration may change according to each particular challenge and the personalities involved in it. The disposition to collaborate seeks an outlet even in difficult circumstances – in fact, that is when collaboration is most important. To have a collaborative disposition requires flexibility of mind and stability of emotions.

The disposition to be strategic

To be strategic is to develop the tendency, when faced with a challenge, to ask oneself questions like: 'Do I need a plan or strategy? Are the demands of this situation like others I have faced in the past and will what I did then help me now?' It means developing a repertoire of moves and sequences of actions that are appropriate to a number of similar situations. These actions may involve thinking strategies to help solve intellectual problems; they may be tactics for a sports match or they may be moves to help one through uncomfortable disagreements with friends or family. When teachers encourage students to extend their range of strategies, they help them to be more successful learners

Coaching is particularly relevant to the development of strategic thinking. The basis of the N-RAIS coaching approach is a process of *feeding forward* and *feeding back*[6] – noticing, imagining, planning, trying out, checking and adjusting. This is a cycle rather than a set of one-directional stages, and the parts of the cycle often overlap. The distance between trying out and checking during writing, for example, is sometimes imperceptibly small.

Feedforward and feedback is a meta-strategy that can incorporate most other strategies. Without the process of feeding forward and feeding back, our use of other strategies can lead to disappointing results. For example, 'stage one' of the strategy often given to students about how to tackle examination questions is: 'first understand what the question means'. But this is, in itself, a problem requiring a strategy. How do you set about understanding what a question means? The answer is by feeding forward and creating possible meanings and then feeding back on which meanings seem most sensible, most likely or the easiest to answer. Then you start to write (feedforward) but you must check to see if what you have written is answering the question-meaning you have decided upon (feedback). You may need to adjust your answer (feedforward) and check again (feedback). Coaching on how to feedforward and feedback in all kinds of learning situations and how to adjust the process to new challenges is very important. Strategies need to be flexible otherwise they lose their usefulness. Many strategies and flow charts for learning (or 'problem-solving') offered to learners are far too cumbersome and inflexible to be useful.

The disposition to be persistent

To be persistent is to see a task through to completion and remain focused. It is to retain optimism in the face of difficulties and to recover from setbacks. In many ways, the other dispositions are dependent on this one. One might argue that all tasks require persistence, although students need to know what persisting means for each kind of pursuit. For writing, it may mean trying out alternative ways of expressing an idea until one is satisfied. For music, it may mean practising a particular fingering on an instrument, hoping that one day awkwardness will turn into fluency. For maths, it means breaking down a large problem into a set of smaller ones, hoping that confusion will slowly dissipate.

Of course, tasks set in schools should be challenging and worthy of persisting with. It is no good setting 100 sums instead of 20 in the belief that we are exercising the disposition of students to persist. The quality or usefulness of tasks is probably more important than the quantity. A question to ask for each task is: 'If a student persists with this, will it lead to further learning, a genuine sense of achievement or the establishment of a useful habit?'

Coaching is one N-RAIS strategy that promotes and nurtures persistence in a planned way. How this is achieved will be the subject of a later chapter. At this point it is enough to say that, when striving for a goal or tackling a challenging task, people benefit from some of the techniques more often offered by sports coaches than teachers. The N-RAIS team has been exploring how some of those techniques can be adapted for use in schools.

The disposition to encourage oneself and others

Although we benefit from the encouragement of others, we must also be disposed to encourage ourselves. A discouraged person is a dependent person. Self-encouraging people will set goals, take worthwhile risks, accept the fact that everyone makes mistakes, accept that they have limitations and avoid blaming others for setbacks. Teachers who encourage students are helping them to become self-encouraging. When a teacher tells a student: 'I know you will meet this challenge. I have faith in you. I know you will do your best,' the student gains the strength and the language to take over and extend her own sphere of self-encouragement. Teachers who want students to become self-encouraging will provide them with opportunities to adopt self-determined goals, support them in taking risks and help them avoid comparing themselves negatively to others.

Encouraging schools will also strive to provide students with opportunities to discover and encourage each other's hopes and goals. Peer culture in school is often quite harsh and judgmental. Yet there are huge benefits in developing a culture of mutual encouragement. According to psychologist Rudolph Dreikurs, humans need encouragement much as plants need water. Dreikurs said: 'We constantly encourage or discourage those around us and thereby contribute materially to their greater or lesser ability to function.'[7]

Indeed, encouragement is a key ingredient of positive personal and professional relationships. The N-RAIS strategies of philosophical enquiry, coaching and the teaching of thinking are seedbeds for encouragement. They also provide opportunities for people to develop intellectual and emotional resources on which to draw when facing doubts and difficulties.

Attending to strategies and skills

The encouragement of positive dispositions is essential. However, it is not sufficient if our goal is to sustain students on the road to persistent and positive self-development. This is the problem with many self-help books and motivational initiatives. They tend to assume that:

- everyone can succeed with anything if they have the right attitude or disposition
- the concept of success is unproblematic

We know that neither of these assumptions is true. Some people lack the talents or skills to make quick progress towards their goals. Others find the values of their advisers conflict with their own. Both these realities undermine the good intentions and nostrums that lie behind many motivational projects. The development of skills, dispositions and values go hand in hand and all can be encouraged.

Any given disposition may require different combinations of skills for its fulfilment in each new context. For positive dispositions to thrive in intellectual contexts, for example, they may need to be supported by skills such as:

- the ability to construct appropriate questions and know how to follow them up
- the ability to use effective tools for enquiry and analysis such as tables, Venn diagrams and MindMaps
- competency in dialogue with others by making moves such as asking for examples or creating alternative explanations

The development of these kinds of intellectual abilities has been the objective of a wide range of initiatives that share the name 'thinking skills'. Some of the most important skills and strategies involve questioning, comparing, visualizing (actions and consequences) and 'feeding forward and feeding back'. The important point to make is that without positive dispositions, students will not use skills and strategies independently. Without skills and strategies, dispositions cannot be sustained. And, without encouragement, neither positive dispositions or abilities can flourish in a growing range of contexts. The combination of people's dispositions, skills and strategies could be called their 'resources' – those things they draw on to help them meet challenges and develop intellectually, emotionally or interpersonally.

Radical Encouragement

We are now ready to offer a definition of Radical Encouragement as 'the deliberate application of multiple strategies by an organisation to encourage the dispositions, strategies and skills necessary for persistent and positive self-development by people within its sphere of influence.'

What any organisation regards as 'positive' rather than 'negative' self-development will vary depending on its purposes. However, persistent self-development is necessarily conceived and carried out willingly because it must express the ambitions and values of an individual human being. A school is a special kind of organisation in that its most important role should be to expand the interests, dispositions and abilities of its students. In educational settings, enabling self-development is not just a means to an end but an end in itself.

Encouragement directs attention away from doing better or worse than others and towards the student's task – to learn.[8] Radical Encouragement helps students to learn better, more independently and in a growing range of contexts. It helps students achieve advancement *in learning* rather than over others in rank order or praise. The N-RAIS strategies aim at starting and supporting a process of Radical Encouragement in schools and the community. Other kinds of activities, strategies and programmes could claim to achieve the same ends. However, as we have seen above, the N-RAIS strategies seem to be particularly suitable for developing the resources (dispositions, skills and strategies) we have in mind.

Development pyramids

The intended effects of Radical Encouragement can be illustrated graphically through the notion of development pyramids.

The base of a pyramid represents a person's current reality, their daily life, their family, friends, culture, interests and past achievements. We could call this their lifeworld. The three sides of the pyramid represent aspirations, resources and encouragement. We start to build a pyramid each time we aspire to try something new or reach for a goal. Our aspiration engages our resources (dispositions, skills and strategies) to meet the challenge. If the resources are not sufficient, encouragement helps us to persist and develop our resources in collaboration with more experienced helpers.

Success is measured by how much our resources have been enhanced, how our reality has been expanded and how far our aspirations have been advanced. Each success – each pyramid – builds on past successes. Aspirations and resources develop together with encouragement as a key component of change. The ultimate aim is that dispositions, skills and strategies are extended to new areas and encouragement strengthens into self-encouragement.

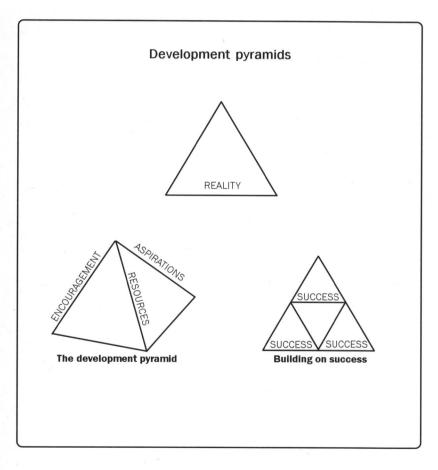

Development pyramids

REALITY

ENCOURAGEMENT
ASPIRATIONS
RESOURCES

The development pyramid

SUCCESS
SUCCESS
SUCCESS

Building on success

The important point to make is that without positive dispositions, students will not use skills and strategies independently. Without skills and strategies, dispositions cannot be sustained. And, without encouragement, neither positive dispositions or abilities can flourish in a growing range of contexts. The combination of people's dispositions, skills and strategies could be called their 'resources' – those things they draw on to help them meet challenges and develop intellectually, emotionally or interpersonally.

The effects of encouragement

There is no doubt that many of the initiatives that have succeeded in changing the lives of students are supported by a culture of constant encouragement. Reuven Feuerstein[9] and his followers, for example, set students simple but sophisticated challenges such as finding patterns in groups of dots. They had faith that students could succeed with these kinds of challenges. They discussed with students the resources (dispositions, skills and strategies) involved in the tasks, such as persistence, suppressing impulsivity, being systematic, noticing similarities and differences and so on. They persuaded students that if they could develop the necessary resources to solve a task with dots they could extend (or 'bridge') them to other ones where they had previously failed. Students were given encouragement and help with each new extension. Feuerstein showed that these kinds of incremental successes can revive students from states of chronic academic failure and discouragement.[10] Yet without large doses of just the right kind of encouragement, the paper exercises with the dots seem very unpromising vehicles through which to instigate student progress.

Matthew Lipman and his colleagues had faith that students from all backgrounds could philosophise together in a 'community of enquiry'. Their programme, *Philosophy for Children*, encouraged many positive dispositions and their faith was rewarded with remarkable results – teachers were shocked by the quality and complexity of their students' thinking.[11] The N-RAIS team has used *Philosophy for Children* as the foundation of its philosophical work with schools in Northumberland and, in so doing, has joined a growing network of educationalists around the world who see the value of philosophical enquiry with children and young people.

How to encourage

Five core techniques for encouraging dispositions, skills and strategies are orchestrating, modelling, reviewing, coaching and promoting.

Orchestrating means ordering and planning the context for encouragement. The essential questions for teachers are: 'What kind of challenges are appropriate? How will I incorporate choice? What support will I give? How will I use students' own interests to energise my teaching? How will I draw attention to dispositions, skills and strategies?'

Modelling means demonstrating the target dispositions, skills and strategies. Teachers show their curiosity, their disposition to review and their strategies for making connections. They show their thought processes in coming to decide that a particular strategy is appropriate for a problem they face with the class. They also model self-encouragement: 'I don't know what to do but I will give it my best effort. Even if I fail, I might learn something. Here goes!'

Reviewing. To review something is to draw attention to it. Teachers not only review their students' accumulation of knowledge and their grades but also the way they think and the dispositions they show. It is heartening, for example, when teachers make time to review the students' levels of curiosity by collecting and studying their questions. It's good to hear comments to a student like: 'I'm impressed you are applying your talent for asking good questions to new lesson topics'.

Promoting means arguing for the value of the target skills, strategies and dispositions. This can often be done by drawing on positive (or negative examples) from fact or fiction and developing inclusive stories (see page 13).

Coaching means offering special attention to individuals or groups to work on building confidence or skills. Coaches sometimes offer students particular techniques they think will help, such as visualizing a successful outcome to a challenge. They almost always communicate faith in their students' capacities to develop skills and dispositions. Coaches help students to evaluate their strengths and assets and define their goals. In the chapters that follow, we will explore some of these techniques of encouragement, using examples from the work of N-RAIS consultants in schools.

Radical Encouragement for teachers

Although the explanation of Radical Encouragement given so far in this chapter stresses what teachers do, it is clear from research and observation that positive outcomes are rarely achieved by coercing teachers into adopting methods they find uncomfortable or disagreeable.

In its work with schools, the N-RAIS team has benefited from being an independent organisation able to offer support to schools free of charge. It has not had to promote officially-sanctioned methods or materials, it has not inspected or judged teachers and it has not pressed them relentlessly to chase government targets – as is often the case with government-funded advisers. Instead, its starting point has been a vision of thoughtful, encouraging educational environments for both teachers and learners. N-RAIS consultants worked together with teachers on ways to create such environments. Courses offered by N-RAIS staff proved immensely popular and influential in changing expectations of teaching and learning. Consultants worked in schools with teachers only when invited to do so. Teachers were never made to feel inadequate or guilty but were listened to, supported and treated with professional respect. Consultants often worked alongside teachers and welcomed feedback on their own performance in the classroom. This positive approach carried over into courses for parents and community groups. The principles and implications of Radical Encouragement provided a starting point for discussion with schools and teachers about goals and possibilities. Methods were not imposed.

At the same time, the N-RAIS team had some strong recommendations about the kinds of strategies that can give a powerful initial boost to the momentum of Radical Encouragement in any school. It is time to look in more detail at philosophical enquiry, teaching thinking skills and coaching. What are they, how do they work and how do they help people to develop positive dispositions, skills and strategies?

2

Philosophy for Children

*P*hilosophy is an academic discipline with an ancient tradition of thinking about thinking. In the form of Philosophy for Children, it has been developed into a method for transforming classrooms into 'communities of enquiry'. Whatever the content of their discussions, communities of enquiry form a supportive context for acquiring thinking skills and positive dispositions. Philosophical discussions within a community of enquiry provide an opportunity for developing conceptual thinking. Perhaps the most distinctive contribution of philosophy is the possibility it offers to help children and young people become active creators of meanings and values. It is a key strategy for Radical Encouragement.

BRENDAN MALKIN, head of Tweedmouth West First School, in Northumberland, realised that she had a problem. A pupil attitude survey had revealed that some boys in year three (aged eight) were not engaging with the school or with their education. The survey, developed and tested by Keele University,[12] asked questions like: 'Do you enjoy helping the teacher?' and 'How do you feel about coming to school?' Brendan had looked at all the answers. While she could have predicted some of the boys who revealed their disaffection with school, others came as a shock. Jimmy, for instance, who always appeared keen to help her set up equipment, was also apparently unhappy and bored with school. Gangs of disaffected boys playing truant and causing trouble were now a serious issue for the nearby middle school. Brendan could see that this would be the fate of her boys unless she did something. She also knew that, in this area of high unemployment, failure at school would probably be just the first in a whole series of failures.

So what did she do? Firstly, the problem was aired in a staff meeting and teachers were issued with a list of those children – all boys – who she felt to be at risk of turning away from their education. The teachers in the school were primed to notice any signs of effort or interest in these boys and to encourage them. However, Brendan felt that this was insufficient. Something more radical was needed. The N-RAIS team had introduced her to *Philosophy for Children* and she decided to try it in this case. She started a philosophy club in the school and invited all the at-risk boys to attend.

It might seem strange to think that philosophy could help to re-engage children who were already becoming estranged from education. In the past, philosophers have been accused of promoting disaffection through asking too many critical questions. But philosophy also has another much more constructive side. Through teaching the art of questioning and the exploration of possible answers, it enables people to create their own meanings and values in collaboration with others.

Brendan Malkin was wise enough to see that her boys were becoming disaffected from education because they experienced it as something that other people were doing to them and not as something that they were doing for themselves. This problem could not be adequately addressed from outside by, for example, giving them more praise if they were good and more blame if they were bad. What was required was a change from within the disaffected boys themselves. Somehow they needed to be encouraged to take charge of their own meaning-making. Philosophy, as practised in the *Philosophy for Children* model taught by the N-RAIS team, might be able to give these children the opportunities and the tools that they needed to question the world and to construct their own meaning within it.

Brendan's strategy worked. The boys took the bait and seriously engaged in creating challenging questions and exploring answers together. Through this they became more involved in their own education. And when, at the end of the year, they went on to the middle school, Brendan had the great satisfaction of seeing them thrive there. She was convinced that without her intervention and use of philosophy the boys would have joined the disaffected sub-culture of the middle school and been destined for educational failure.

Philosophy seemed not only to have helped children develop useful skills and positive dispositions, it also helped them change their stories about themselves. They became, in their own minds, 'philosophers' – and philosophers are capable of thinking with discrimination about problems. By affecting skills, dispositions and self-stories, philosophy has become an indispensable tool for Radical Encouragement.

What is Philosophy for Children?

Philosophy for Children (P4C) was first developed by philosophy professor Matthew Lipman and his associates at Montclair State College, New Jersey, in the USA. SAPERE, the organisation for *Philosophy for Children* in the UK, provides the following history: [13]

Lipman's aim was to encourage young people to be more reasonable – that is, ready to reason and be reasoned with. Like the ancient Greek philosophers, he saw this as the path to the ultimate goal of education: 'practical wisdom' or good judgement.

Lipman emphasised the importance of questioning and enquiry in the development of reasoning. He also appreciated from Lev Vygotsky, the Russian psychologist, that we learn to think much as we learn to speak – by internalising the patterns of speech that we hear around us. Thinking for ourselves is, at least in part, borrowing the language of others to talk to ourselves.

Putting these educational insights together, Lipman developed a model of learning – *Communities of Inquiry* (using the American spelling of 'Inquiry') – in which teachers and children collaborate with each other to grow in understanding of the material, personal and ethical worlds around them.

Philosophy seemed not only to have helped children develop useful skills and positive dispositions, it also helped them change their stories about themselves. They became, in their own minds, 'philosophers' – and philosophers are capable of thinking with discrimination about problems. By affecting skills, dispositions and self-stories, philosophy has become an indispensable tool for Radical Encouragement.

Philosophy for Children was originally conceived as a separate subject. However, *Community of Inquiry* is also a method which can be used in any curriculum area. Questions leading to philosophical enquiry could be replaced by questions leading to historical or scientific enquiry.

Lipman wrote his own materials to support philosophical enquiry in classrooms but the essential method is very flexible. In the UK, it is common to use picture books, news stories or works of art as stimuli for enquiry. Despite this flexibility, all P4C sessions follow certain principles and procedures. Some key tenets include:

- valuing each person's interests and questions
- valuing knowledge but also questioning certainty
- appreciating different ways of interpreting and thinking

Such principles are sometimes translated into negotiated ground rules, such as 'not putting each other down', or 'giving each speaker time to finish', which are then given prominence as the ground rules for talking in a class.

In addition, *Philosophy for Children* includes some of the tools and dispositions which have always been characteristic of philosophy, including, as Laurance Splitter[14] writes:

- the skills of argument (such as forming conclusions, identifying premises, deductive and non-deductive thinking, exposing poor reasoning and striving for consistency)
- a propensity to question and search for reasons, rather than simply accept what is given
- identifying, applying and modifying the criteria by which we make decisions and form judgements (including value judgements)
- making distinctions that allow us to see the complexity of things (focusing on the nuanced 'grey' areas that always lie between the black and the white)
- identifying relationships that help us make sense of things (including relations of, similarity and difference, cause and effect, means and ends, parts and wholes, centre and periphery and so on)

- exercising empathy and imagination by contemplating different ways of proceeding, and representing alternative moral positions and world views (the 'what if ...?' strategy).

Philosophy is sometimes seen as a form of critical reasoning, employing cold logic alone. That is certainly one style of doing philosophy but Lipman's approach is to promote discussions which are *critical*, *caring* and *creative* in equal parts. To come up with analogies or ways of seeing that unpack the meaning of an issue is highly creative. The very act of having a dialogue with others requires us to care about issues and to care for each other. A community of enquiry is a supportive social space where children are able to risk articulating their ideas and emotions.

Philosophy for Children at Tweedmouth West First School

Encouraged and supported by the N-RAIS team, Brendan Malkin and her teachers all took short training courses provided by N-RAIS team members in *Philosophy for Children* and this influenced the way that they taught every subject area.[15] She also cleared time to focus entirely on philosophy. This is what she called the *Philosophy Club*.

The teacher provided an initial stimulus to start off each philosophy session. The nature of this varied greatly: sometimes it was a walk outside, sometimes a news item, a picture, a story or a video clip. The children then had to think of a good question to ask. They did this individually, in pairs or in small groups. All the questions were written up and considered in turn. The children were then asked to decide on the question that they wanted to consider first by voting.

When engaged in philosophy, the children sit in a circle so they can all see each other. The teacher's interventions do not focus so much on the content of the discussion as on the quality of the thinking. *Philosophy for Children* aims to develop understanding and good judgement through critical examination of *meanings* of words, *facts* of the matter, personal *feelings*, *views* and *values*.

Training in *Philosophy for Children* equips teachers with the strategies to manage the children's dialogues and to model the sort of language that supports reflection. Some of the questions a teacher uses, and encourages the children to use, reveal the thinking skills that are being modelled:

- questions (what don't we understand here? what questions do we have about this?)
- hypotheses (does anyone have any alternative suggestions or explanations?)
- reasons (what reasons are there for doing that? or evidence for believing this?)
- examples (can anyone think of an example of this? or a counter-example?)
- distinctions (can we make a distinction here? or give a definition?)
- connections (is anyone able to build on that idea? or link it with another?)
- implications (what assumptions lie behind this? what consequences does it lead to?)
- intentions (is that what was really meant? is that what we're really saying?)
- criteria (what makes that an example of X? what are the things that really count here?)
- consistency (does that conclusion follow? are these principles/beliefs consistent?)[16]

The model questions suggested in the parentheses above are used by the teacher to guide the children to appropriate this kind of questioning for themselves. Over a year, Brendan Malkin noticed this process working. She kept a record of the questions that her year three children formulated in their philosophy club. They began the year often asking rather superficial questions of the kind: 'What did the dinosaur have for lunch?' but they ended the year asking far deeper questions such as: 'What is 'thinking'?' or 'What makes people happy?'

We interviewed some of the children from her philosophy club. They told us that they enjoyed the opportunity to talk with their peers and that they also often talked about the topic of the philosophy session later that day with their parents at home. One eight-year-old girl told us that her experience of philosophy gave her much greater confidence to speak out in many situations. She told us how someone in the last philosophy club session had suggested that they ask why, in the story book under discussion, the Little Polar Bear had followed the Captain. She had responded that first they had to clarify what they meant by 'follow' because, she explained, 'follow' did not always mean walking behind someone.

As well as helping her disaffected boys, Brendan Malkin found that philosophy also helped her 'quiet, shy girls' who were never any trouble in class nor overtly disaffected in any way, but who did not push forward with their learning. They seemed happy to concentrate instead on the neat presentation of their work. The emphasis on 'listening with respect' in the philosophy club helped these quiet pupils, giving them the support that they needed to ask questions and express views.

Brendan was particularly proud when a mother and father came to thank her for the transformation that they had seen in their daughter. They had been worried about how timid she had been and her inability to face challenges but somehow, in the words of her parents: 'the school had given her what she needed to make a go of things'. Once again, Brendan could see that the philosophy sessions had made a difference.

The dispositions and skills developed by Philosophy for Children

The example given above of disaffected boys changing their attitude to education illustrates how central *Philosophy for Children* is to the Radical Encouragement approach. Philosophy has the potential to enable children to become more confident makers of meaning in school and in their own lives. But, as we have argued, the Radical Encouragement approach is not only about giving confidence, it is also about equipping learners with the tools that they need to succeed and changing their self-stories – but how?

Philosophy for Children works by drawing children into the practice of reasoning together which they then internalise or appropriate into individual reasoning skills and dispositions. Matthew Lipman suggested[17] that, through philosophical dialogue, pupils learn to:

- formulate questions
- avoid sweeping generalisations
- ask that claims be supported by evidence
- develop explanatory hypotheses
- recognise situational differences
- build on the ideas of others
- accept reasonable criticisms
- welcome hearing 'the other side of the case'
- respect others as persons
- offer appropriate analogies
- seek to clarify ill-defined concepts
- make relevant distinctions and connections
- support opinions with convincing reasons
- provide examples and counter-examples
- seek to uncover underlying assumptions
- draw suitable inferences
- make balanced evaluative judgements

It is noticeable that many of these are not so much 'cognitive skills', important as these are, but 'dispositions'. For example, *Philosophy for Children* develops the dispositions of questioning, listening carefully and empathetically to an alternative point of view and persevering with a problem. Such dispositions cannot be taught without engaging in dialogue any more than swimming can be taught without entering the water. *Philosophy for Children* sessions provide a context for practising good thinking moves so that they can become embedded as dispositions that the children will carry away with them. Those who have taken part in philosophical dialogues for any length of time often find, for example, that they can no longer accept many of the claims that are made every day on the TV or in the newspapers without questioning the assumptions behind them and seeking to find alternative perspectives and counter-examples. They may also find themselves uncomfortable with the easy dismissal of alternative perspectives through caricature and labelling. It is likely also that they develop pleasure in pursuing challenging problems to a satisfactory conclusion.

Brendan was particularly proud when a mother and father came to thank her for the transformation that they had seen in their daughter. They had been worried about how timid she had been and her inability to face challenges but somehow, in the words of her parents: 'the school had given her what she needed to make a go of things'. Once again, Brendan could see that the philosophy sessions had made a difference.

As well as developing positive dispositions for learning, *Philosophy for Children* imparts some quite specific skills and strategies such as how to formulate good questions, how to apply criteria in making judgements and how to offer reasons. In philosophy, students not only apply these skills and strategies but they learn to do so reflectively and self-consciously, with a view to evaluating how well a given strategy is employed. So, for example, teachers teach children to reason but they also show them how to distinguish good reasons from bad ones, and encourage them to value the good ones. The same process is applied to other thinking strategies such as using analogies and generating hypotheses.

Verification of this comes from a recent inspection (OfSTED) report on Tweedmouth West First School which states:

> 'A significant proportion of pupils start school with below average language and communication skills. The development of pupils' speaking skills is very good throughout the school and pupils achieve very well. The introduction of 'thinking skills' and 'philosophy for children' are having a significant impact. For example, many pupils will qualify an answer to a question with a reason; this effectively develops their oral communication skills. In all classes good use is made of 'talking partners' which encourages pupils to discuss their ideas before sharing them with the class and develops their confidence in speaking.'

Key words and key moves

Much skill in thinking can be observed in the way that key words and patterns of words are deployed. Laurance Splitter[18] argues that:

> It is one thing to ask questions of the form 'Why...?', 'What if....?', 'Do you agree?' and so on. What coaching in philosophical enquiry generates beyond this is an appreciation that these questions are prompts for reasons, predictions and viewpoints which can, in turn, be evaluated as good or bad, better or worse, reasonable or unreasonable. Philosophical thinking requires an understanding of such concepts as *reason* (and what constitutes a *good reason*). Through *Philosophy for Children*, students become skilled in

using a vocabulary of essential *words for thinking* such as: reason, reasonable, criteria, meaning, concept, judgment, question, assumption, distinction, relationship, analogy, inference, example, counter-example, evidence, consistent, true, good, ethical, logical.

An understanding of the concepts that lie behind these words provides learners with resources which equip them to manage virtually any enquiry they might face. These resources, like the dispositions mentioned earlier, are something that children and young people can take away with them from the classroom to apply in real-life situations.

Big concepts and values

Philosophy for Children discussions tend to focus on concepts of significant that are interesting to children such as:

fairness, justice, friendship, rights, love, identity, knowledge, truth, belief, belonging and free will.

Thinking about why these concepts recur as the subjects of philosophical enquiry – both throughout history and now in the school classroom – Laurance Splitter draws our attention to three specific features.[19] These concepts are, he claims:

- *Common* to the experiences of all – or most – thinking beings, including children (they are not remote or esoteric; most people can relate both to the concepts and the experiences they involve).
- *Central* to the way we understand or make sense of our experience (they function as bridges or vehicles of thought, the entities by means of which thought is carried on).
- *Contestable* or problematic (they resist our best attempts to define them with complete clarity and finality).

The centrality of these concepts to many debates in a range of contexts is one reason why reflection on these concepts, and skill in discussing them, can transfer beyond the classroom community of enquiry.

Philosophy and higher-order thinking

Lauren Resnick, a well-known American educationalist, was asked by the US government to chair a major enquiry into the nature and value of teaching thinking skills. Her final report contained a widely-quoted account of the nature of 'Higher-Order Thinking Skills'.[20] In fact, her account reads like a list of the features of a successful community of enquiry. According to Resnick, higher-order thinking:

- is *non algorithmic*. That is, the path of action is not fully specified in advance
- tends to be *complex*. The total path is not 'visible' (mentally speaking) from any single vantage point
- often yields *multiple solutions*, each with costs and benefits, rather than unique solutions
- involves *nuanced judgement* and interpretation
- involves the application of *multiple criteria*, which sometimes conflict with one another
- often involves *uncertainty*. Not everything that bears on the task at hand is known
- involves *self-regulation* of the thinking process. We do not recognise higher-order thinking in an individual when someone else 'calls the plays' at every step
- involves *imposing meaning*, finding structure in apparent disorder
- is *effortful*. There is considerable mental work involved in the kinds of elaborations and judgements required

Resnick describes these as if they were the characteristics of a certain type of thought – higher-order thought – but in working communities of enquiry these are the characteristics of a way of talking. The term 'higher-order thinking skills' is normally used as a contrast with 'lower-order thinking skills', described in Bloom's taxonomy[21] as skills such as 'comprehension' and 'memorisation'. Some people think that the lower skills should be taught first as a basis for the higher skills.

This is not the point of view taken by Matthew Lipman, founder of *Philosophy for Children*. He points out that, just because wholes are capable of being analysed into parts, it does not follow that the assemblage of parts must precede the construction of wholes. The philosophy method is to induct children directly into the highest possible forms of thinking in the belief that all the necessary individual skills will follow from this.

Evaluating Philosophy for Children

It is notoriously difficult to evaluate the success of thinking skills programmes partly because they aim at teaching skills that 'transfer' to new contexts. However, a serious evaluation undertaken for Clackmannanshire Council in Scotland indicates that *Philosophy for Children* can deliver measurable gains.[22] Interviewed about his report, Professor Keith Topping of the University of Dundee explained:

> 'Some educators argue that improvement in thinking is impossible to measure. However, this review identified 10 rigorous controlled experimental studies of P4C. These studies measured outcomes by norm-referenced tests of reading, reasoning, cognitive ability and other curriculum-related abilities, by measures of self-esteem and child behaviour, and by child and teacher questionnaires. All studies showed some positive outcomes and a consistent moderate positive effect size for P4C on a wide range of outcome measures. This suggests a gain in IQ of 6.5 points for an average child.'[23]

Inspectors' reports provide an unbiased insight into what is actually happening in schools that have taken up *Philosophy for Children*. Recent reports on several schools in the N-RAIS area seem to back up the claim that *Philosophy for Children* really does develop children's resources for learning.

'Learning is particularly strong in lessons in which pupils take a leading role. The 'philosophy for children' programme is helping pupils to develop their own questions, which they attempt to answer through high quality discussion and debate. For example, in an excellent Year 3 lesson, pupils posed some outstanding questions about a box the teacher held, that helped them to make inferences and to deduce exceptionally well. In other lessons, pupils think of questions to ask whilst working and these are displayed on a board ready for discussion. In some classes, the 'display committee' consult with other classmates as to which questions to include on displays. This is a very good example of the philosophy for children programme, which gives pupils a thirst for learning.' (OfSTED report on Seaton Sluice First School, March 2005)

'Pupils are challenged to think and develop enquiry skills. Lessons are characterised by their practical nature. In all the lessons observed, pupils were challenged to formulate relevant questions in order to solve scientific problems. The development of philosophy is helping pupils to develop greater understanding in how to plan investigations, as well as enabling them to improve their enquiry skills.' (OfSTED report on Tweedmouth West First School, June 2005)

'The school has an uplifting ethos. Pupils learn considerable respect for others, as well as for themselves. Pupils are encouraged to reflect on a variety of issues. In philosophy lessons, where pupils are encouraged to develop a breadth of thinking, pupils look at abstract photographs to stimulate conversation as pupils consider what they might mean.' (OfSTED report on Holy Trinity Church of England (VA) First School, Berwick-upon-Tweed, December 2005)

'In a Year 6 lesson in philosophy for children, pupils showed an above average competence for their age in their capacity to explore what makes for a happy person ... which contributed well to the development of their thinking skills and capacity to co-operate effectively with each other.' (OfSTED report on Tweedmouth Middle School, May 2005)

Thinking skills and dialogues

Thinking skills are often seen as the property of individuals and it is true, in a sense, that thinking is something that goes on inside an individual's brain. So how does engaging in philosophical dialogues influence the development of individual thinking? The Russian psychologist, Lev Vygotsky, suggested an answer when he wrote in the 1920s that 'all that is internal in the higher mental functions was at one time external'.[24] His claim, one we have mentioned earlier, is that the intellectual performance of an individual may have its roots in their prior social experience. More precisely, he argued that psychological capacities are created by the 'internalisation' of social activity. For example, he argues that the process of silent reflection is an internalised version of talk, by which the individual can conduct an inner dialogue. Thinking goes on in the brain but the brain turns out to be a very flexible organ that can be shaped by our habits. Guy Claxton writes about this process, describing how activities such as engaging in dialogue with others gradually shape what he calls our 'brainscape'.[25] This same argument can be applied to the relationship between reasoning in conversations and the development of individual reason. That is, individual reasoning is an internalisation of collective reasoning in a dialogue.

Research in psychology tends to confirm that thought, creative thought as well as critical reasoning and problem-solving, develops through engagement in dialogues. Psychologist Peter Hobson,[26] for example, argues that early dialogues open up what he calls a 'mental space' which then becomes internalised in consciousness. His point is that in a dialogue, even in non-verbal peek-a-boo games, children learn that things can be seen in different ways from different perspectives. In fact, to be aware of something at all is to see it as if from the perspective of other people and so to be potentially able to express it and to share it with other people. A capacity to engage effectively in dialogue with other people, and with tasks, appears to lie behind many of the techniques, habits and dispositions referred to in the literature on thinking skills. Higher-order thinking skills, such as reasoning, evaluating, reflective self-monitoring and ordering information, all appear to originate in the context of dialogues.

Philosophy and older students: an example

Earlier, we described how philosophy worked to engage potentially difficult and disaffected pupils in a first school but philosophy and the community of enquiry approach to learning can work well with any age group. In a community college in Blythe, teachers were particularly impressed with the way that the community of enquiry transformed teaching and learning on their A-Level business studies course. One of the teachers commented:

> 'We used to give them reading to do and then ask them questions. With the community of enquiry we turned that around, we got them to read together and come up with questions, trying to come up with deeper questions, and then voting on which question to discuss. They really liked this because it gave them ownership of their learning and we think it transformed the teaching – it was much better.'

He went on to give a specific example of the kind of 'ridiculous' question that the children could come up with. They were looking at statistical correlation as applied to business – for example, the correlation between profit and advertising costs. Often this is complex and indirect due to the many variables involved. One student put forward a question for discussion: 'Is there a correlation between height and distance from the equator?' Her justification for asking this question was that height might be linked to the amount of sunlight people receive and since there is, she said, more sunlight near the equator then people there should be taller. The teacher said that even though this question was not directly relevant to business studies, nonetheless students learnt a great deal about correlations by discussing it – and all that they learnt could be applied later in the course.

Like Brendan Malkin, the teacher was impressed with the way this technique increased the participation of students. One girl was very quiet at the start of her A-level business studies course. She did not speak unless directly questioned. But once the teacher tried the community of enquiry approach she began to speak much more, offering her opinions and engaging in debates. His view was that she had been worried about speaking before because she felt under pressure to give the right answer. However, as the ethos of a community of enquiry became established, her confidence grew. She felt more able to participate. The teacher referred to another girl who always thought she was right and annoyed the group by dominating discussions. The community of enquiry approach, especially through the stress it lays on careful listening to the views of others, helped this girl to became a constructive participant.

These two cases illustrate a general and important shift in focus that all the teachers in Blythe Community College noticed. Instead of competing to be first to answer correctly or striving to anticipate what teachers wanted them to say, students began to approach questions differently. They started to discuss issues with each other and with the teacher. It took a while for this to happen but when it did it brought about a different attitude to learning. The students felt more empowered and engaged. Through selecting the questions for debate, they felt that they had some ownership over what they were learning.

In fact, the teachers influenced the discussion and the learning that ensued, leading the children towards topics that they had to cover for the curriculum. However, this did not lessen students' feelings that they were in charge of their own learning to a far greater extent than before.

Giving students the responsibility for devising questions paid off in other ways as well. Several teachers noticed that behaviour in class had improved. One teacher pointed out that while there was always one 'silly' or destructive question, the class never voted for that one. Other teachers contributed stories of two disruptive boys, known to the whole school, who had been transformed by the philosophy sessions. It seems that part of the reason these students had been challenging previously had been their desire to be heard. The community of enquiry provided an opportunity for them to speak and put their point of view in a constructive way. In a community of enquiry, responsibility for self-regulation shifts from the teacher to the whole group. The social pressure on individuals to behave in a responsible and constructive way becomes very strong. Difficult students, who did not change their behaviour in the face of threats from authority figures, responded very differently when faced with the opinion of their peers that they were being disruptive.

Summary

The central aim of Radical Encouragement is to help turn people away from feeling like passive spectators of life to becoming active creators of their own meanings and capable of learning and developing. Philosophy is not formally required by the curriculum and many teachers would see the idea of teaching philosophy as interesting but not central to meeting the educational needs of children. But the experiences of teachers in the N-RAIS project indicate that philosophy can indeed be central because it contributes so much to helping pupils develop resources for learning and positive dispositions.

Despite all the government papers that suggest otherwise, some of the most important problems in education are not technical but philosophical ones. For young people, the question is not so much *how* to learn but *why*? Philosophy helps them think about this question and enables them to experience the pleasures of thinking for themselves.

3

Coaching

*Coaching is a form of intensive, planned encouragement targeted at the develop-
ment of positive dispositions and personal resources. In this chapter, we discuss the
concept of coaching and report on ways that N-RAIS consultants have used coaching
techniques to help pupils in schools and people in local communities.*

THE CONCEPT OF COACHING is most associated with sport. Football teams
have coaches – as do tennis players and athletes. In recent times, however, we hear more about coaches in other areas of life: there are voice
coaches, acting coaches and even tidiness coaches. What, then, are the
qualities that might prompt us to use the term 'coaching' about some
kinds of personal interactions?

The most familiar function of a coach is to prepare someone for an
event or role. In sport, the coach prepares competitors for tournaments.
This can involve not only working on vital skills and strategies but also
on positive attitudes and self-confidence. So sportsmen and women
are regularly asked by their coaches to visualize their own good performance, stick with simple goals and talk positively to themselves rather
than 'go negative' and allow their self-belief to drain away.

Coaching in other areas of life is not so different. If we employ someone to help us get our house tidy, then that 'tidiness coach' will introduce us to some simple skills and strategies for cleaning with the most effective products and tools. The more important challenge, however, will be to help us set goals for regular cleaning and sustain our belief that we can achieve them. Coaching, then, is about working with people to set and achieve goals through the development of skills, strategies and positive dispositions. Coaching aims towards independent performance – when sportspeople perform at an event they perform alone and when the tidiness coach leaves their clients must keep the house in order with no external pressure.

We usually associate coaching with individuals or small groups of people who willingly work with a coach because they already have a specific goal – to become good tennis players or to give up smoking. However, it is now common for people to ask others to help them reflect on more existential goals and support them through a positive change in the direction of their lives. The helper or 'life coach' will, in common with other coaches, offer techniques, strategies and, perhaps most importantly, a listening ear to the client.

Finally, coaches provide a safe and supportive environment for risk-taking – that essential element of all change. They do this through drawing attention to people's existing strengths and resources. Thus coaches encourage their clients to leave their 'comfort zones' and their fears behind and strive towards their goals: to learn a new golf stroke, speak in public or lessen their financial debts. Coaches support clients with continuous cycles of *feedforward* and *feedback*. Feedforward involves setting goals, planning strategies, visualizing successes and having a go. Feedback involves evaluating performances and replanning. Coaching always involves these two processes. When the feeding back and adjusting processes are absent, as they are in many self-help books, then coaching will be less effective. It is also important that the values implicit in any coaching approach are open to question and dialogue. In the following parts of the chapter, we assess the potential for coaching relationships in education and local communities illustrated by the work of N-RAIS.

Coaching in education

Teaching inevitably involves an aspect of coaching. Teachers are often able to grab moments with individual pupils to work on a skill here or encourage a positive attitude there. The teaching of study and exam techniques also exemplifies coaching for a particular event or purpose. And, of course, effective teachers draw attention to the strengths and resources of their students, always trying to provide opportunities for achievements. Yet the opportunities teachers have for encouragement through coaching will always be limited. They work with large groups of pupils who are not often united in common goals of learning. Is there anything practical, then, for teachers to learn from the techniques of successful coaches? The work of N-RAIS consultants suggests that there is. Their approach was based on five key principles:

- Create opportunities to listen to what students have to say about their lives, aspirations and fears.
- Create more instances or moments of encouragement through coaching by planning them into the school calendar.
- Maximise the impact of those moments by anchoring them in the minds of students through photographs, lists (or 'anchor charts'), diaries and other kinds of reminders.
- Teach students some techniques of self-encouragement and provide opportunities for them to coach and encourage others.
- Encourage pupils to take more responsibility and coach them to make the most of it.

N-RAIS consultants offer coaching ideas based on these principles to teachers and, together, they negotiate a project or initiative to try out with pupils. We describe some examples below.

The 'Outsmart Day'

Outsmart is an event based around a series of outdoor experiences. It can last for a single day or a whole week. Many Northumberland schools have undertaken a one-day event outdoors with the help of N-RAIS. These *Outsmart Days* provide opportunities for coaching pupils in many of the dispositions, skills and strategies they will need for persistent and positive self-development. The day is not only a valuable event in its own right, it also provides an anchor for the discussion and development of personal resources long after the day is over. What then do pupils do on an *Outsmart Day*?

Several weeks before the event, N-RAIS consultants visit the school and talk with teachers about the principles behind the day and the personal resources pupils will be encouraged to use. The latter are open to negotiation but the most popular requests from teachers are for experiences that develop:

- collaboration, dialogue and reflection
- peer encouragement of others, particularly of those who are reluctant to have a go
- strategic thinking when faced with problems

Teachers prepare pupils for the day by, for example, asking them to think of a time they collaborated: 'What worked well? What were the problems? Did you try any ways to overcome the problems? When you work with people in the future what might you do differently?' Of course, questions about encouragement will also come up: 'Can you remember a time when someone encouraged you? How did they do that? What did they say or do? How did they make you feel? Can you remember a time when you encouraged someone else? How did that make *you* feel?'

In this way, pupils are prompted to reflect on their previous experiences in order to prepare them for some of the challenges ahead. Often they gather together phrases of praise and encouragement such as: *keep going, come on,* and *brilliant.* They may play a simple game prompting them to use their encouragement vocabulary and then reflect on how it felt to be encouraged. This is all part of a long-term aim for them to encourage themselves and others. It is worth quoting Rudolph Dreikurs again: 'We constantly encourage or discourage those around us and thereby contribute materially to their greater or lesser ability to function.'[27]

When the *Outsmart Day* arrives, pupils spend time in the open air enjoying a series of challenges with frequent pauses for reflection and discussion. They are split into three teams and begin with a series of short activities to establish connections to other people in the team. They reflect on questions such as: 'What makes a good team? How will we get organised? How can we try to improve our performance as the day goes along?' When faced with the last question, pupils usually come up with a strategy that includes the stages of *doing, rethinking* and *changing,* an application of the principle of *feedforward* and *feedback.* They make cards and charts to remind themselves of their questions and conclusions. They design a team logo and a set of team slogans (the first challenge for their collaborative abilities).

It is important to stress that the pupils' questions are often as important as their conclusions. A person's ability to ask the right kinds of questions in the right contexts and then act on them is vital for independent learning. Although the adults raise most of the questions during the first *Outsmart Day*, pupils will become familiar with them. So, for instance, a crucial question for collaboration is: 'how will we get organised?' The conclusion will always depend to some extent on relationships between people in a specific group. In collaborative activities following the *Outsmart Day*, pupils will be asked to come up themselves with the right kinds of questions.

The core of the day involves three challenges. The teams tackle each one in turn and then review the strategies they used and the quality of their collaboration. Here, the central questions are often: 'How did our strategy work? Did we change anything as we went along? How did we collaborate? Could we do better? Did we encourage each other?' Two pupils in each team have special roles that are particularly significant for the review process. One is a 'camera operator' and the other an 'observer'. The observer notes down instances of those positive behaviours identified by the children during their introductory task. The camera operator takes digital photographs of team members working together, achieving tasks and enjoying themselves. The pictures will be used later as 'anchors' to positive aspects of the day. We can think of the word 'anchor' in a coaching context as words, images, sounds or objects that remind people of how they thought, felt or acted in the past. Anchors help pupils recall applying positive dispositions, skills and strategies. They may help pupils to believe they can apply them again in different contexts. After reviewing their responses to one challenge, pupils are asked to prepare a short coaching programme for teams about to tackle the same challenge after them. A review of what makes an effective coach is carried out at the end of the day. The challenges that children undertake on an *Outsmart Day* combine strategic thinking with some physical activity. We give three examples of typical challenges below. They are suitable for children of five and upwards.

Crocodile swamp

Pupils have three crates and two planks of wood. Their task is to transport all members of their team from one point to another across 'the swamp' in not more than 30 minutes. There are two simple rules:

* Only crates can touch the swamp.
* If a person or plank touches the swamp, then the team must start again from the beginning.

Down the drain

Pupils have two buckets of water – one full and one empty. They have six pipes and a jug. Their task is to transfer as much water as possible from the full bucket to the empty one in 30 minutes. The rules are:

- Buckets must stay still.
- The jug must stay near to the full bucket.
- Pipes should only be moved when they are empty.

Toxic toffees

Pupils are faced with two pots in the middle of a rope circle. One pot is filled with 'toffees' which, according to the instructions, are contaminated. In not more than 30 minutes, pupils must transfer these toxic toffees into a 'decontamination pot' using a rope and hook. The rules are:

- Use only the rope and hook to move the toffees.
- No-one is allowed to enter the rope circle.

Outsmart procedures

For each challenge, pupils may make some decisions to affect the level of difficulty. For instance, they can decide the width of the crocodile swamp and the exclusion zone around the toxic toffees. Thus, they are encouraged to push themselves but not beyond their capabilities. When pupils have completed all the challenges and coached other groups they review the entire day. The review session is guided by questions to focus attention on dispositions and strategies: 'What did we persist with? How did it feel when we persisted and worked through a problem? Did we have to review how a strategy was working and change it? How did we collaborate? What did we do to encourage others?' Again, pupils note important questions and conclusions from their discussions.

These will be taken back to the classroom to become 'anchor charts' – reminders to prompt future discussions about dispositions and strategies with which to tackle different kinds of challenges. Also, importantly, the pupils are asked to link their efforts on the *Outsmart Day* to other areas of their lives: 'When is it hard to persist in lessons? When we're stuck with something, would it help to remember how good it feels to work through a problem? Would it help to prompt ourselves with questions about what strategy to try? Did we learn anything about collaboration that we could apply at home or at school?'

Outsmart is an interesting application of coaching techniques in schools. It exemplifies the strategy of maximising the impact of positive moments by anchoring them in the minds of students through photographs, anchor charts, diaries and continuing discussion. Without this important follow-up work (similar to the 'bridging' of thinking skills to a variety of contexts), the day itself would have much less value.

One possible disadvantage of having a set of photographs showing positive examples of collaboration outdoors is that some pupils might look at them fondly and contrast these challenges they enjoyed with less satisfying academic work they do in lessons. Therefore, teachers will often take photographs of positive moments during collaborative academic work. They ask pupils to label the images with ideas about what makes collaboration on academic tasks successful.

Working with teachers and pupils

N-RAIS consultants usually work with pupils on the first *Outsmart Day*. Teachers watch and help. If teachers see the value of the day they can take a course with N-RAIS[28] and carry out future *Outsmart Days* independently. They may also set up some mini *Outsmart* events with pupils over the course of a term. These 'brain breaks', lasting only part of a day, involve a couple of challenges and some targeted coaching on dispositions and skills negotiated beforehand with the class.

Pupils usually enjoy their *Outsmart Days* very much. It is always good to do something different once in a while – particularly in the open air. Yet *Outsmart Days* are obviously more than just pleasant diversions from the regular curriculum. They help to develop many of the dispositions targeted by Radical Encouragement such as being adventurous, collaborative, dialogical, imaginative, reflective, persistent and encouraging. Pupils are coached in some specific techniques such as questioning and changing tactics after review. To gain maximum benefit from the day the pupils need reminders of what they learnt. After they return to the normal school timetable, teachers continue to draw their attention to the dispositions and strategies using the anchor charts that were created on the *Outsmart Day* with the overall aim of extending them to a wider range of contexts.

In the classroom

Nicola Dixon is a teacher at Tweedmouth Middle School in Berwick. When her class of 10-year-olds were enjoying an *Outsmart Day*, she noticed that two boys who had previously been subdued in class were now impressing other children with their persistence and leadership. The boys had previously struggled with both literacy and sport. During the *Outsmart Day*, however, they were able to suggest sensible strategies and they responded well to feedback from others. This gave them a new respect amongst their peers. The qualities they showed became a topic for class discussion, during which Nicola could ask questions like: 'How can we give people more opportunities to show these qualities in class? What would I need to do? What would you need to do? Do good leaders have to be good at everything?'

Children completed their anchor charts of questions and conclusions which remained on the classroom wall for the rest of the year. The conclusions included statements such as: 'to make a good team you need to get along with everyone in your group'. Their 'top tips' revealed an emphasis on listening. In continuing discussions throughout the year, pupils agreed that listening is the key to tackling a challenge together and that if you are on your own you have to listen carefully to your own inner voice. Nicola reports that a common argument from children was: 'if you can stand back and listen then you're going to plan better and get on better'. The anchor charts included other top tips on co-operation, respect and learning from each other. Team slogans created on the *Outsmart Day* were also displayed on the classroom wall: 'Stay happy, never give up.' 'Nothing is impossible.' The anchor charts were accompanied by photographs of children behaving in positive ways: collaborating, listening and being absorbed in a task. In the weeks that followed, the charts and photographs stimulated a lot of discussion. The *Outsmart Day* had helped to create a classroom culture of listening, collaboration and reciprocal encouragement.

This collaborative culture was reinforced in Nicola's class by regular sessions of philosophical enquiry, which also requires the exercise of positive dispositions. In addition, philosophy enables children to enquire more deeply into the nature of qualities such as collaboration, persistence and encouragement. These positive words can easily become slogans ('Be persistent!') that have little meaning or efficacy. Pupils need opportunities to discuss the complexities of concepts such as persistence. They must face questions like: 'Are there circumstances in which giving up is exactly the right thing to do?'

These kinds of questions reflect realities that cannot be ignored because they arise out of variations in people's abilities, priorities and values. If such questions are not aired and discussed by teachers and pupils together then, and not for the first time, realities will undermine good intentions. This is often one of the problems of the self-help book. It disregards reality by trying to impose a 'winner' profile on readers that rarely captures people's imaginations for long because it is either impractical or unappealing.

Effects of Outsmart

By sustaining the culture of encouragement and collaboration set in motion by the *Outsmart Day* and by deepening children's understanding of concepts with regular philosophy sessions, Nicola was able to see real improvements. She tells the story of one pupil, Janet, who revealed serious problems with her sight: 'When I have to climb a rope or catch a ball in PE,' she said, 'I see two of everything.' After discussing the best way to encourage people with physical disabilities in a philosophy session, the class attitude towards her changed. From then on, whenever she delayed an activity in PE, she received encouragement rather than groans from her peers. It appears from this, and other illustrations offered to us by teachers, that coaching and philosophical enquiry work together to support a positive culture for learning.

Coaching school councils

Carol Oliver, headteacher of Horton Grange First School, asked for help from N-RAIS consultants with a special coaching task – to set up a school council and help children fulfil the roles of class representatives. She and the governors wanted children to be more involved in school decision-making. At the same time, the school had been bequeathed £1,000. She thought a forum of children should decide how the money could be spent on improving playground facilities. Planning for a school council began. She thought it would be an exciting experiment in encouraging children to take responsibility for school-wide decision-making. She trusted them to make good judgements.

First of all, N-RAIS staff supported teachers at the school in the task of working with children to decide how the school council would run. Pupils had to answer questions like:

- How would all children be represented?
- How would representatives be chosen?
- How would the council conduct its business?
- How would decisions be made?
- How would council members report back to classes?

Pupils need opportunities to discuss the complexities of concepts such as persistence. They must face questions like: 'Are there circumstances in which giving up is exactly the right thing to do?' These kinds of questions reflect realities that cannot be ignored because they arise out of variations in people's abilities, priorities and values. If such questions are not aired and discussed by teachers and pupils together then, and not for the first time, realities will undermine good intentions. This is often one of the problems of the self-help book. It disregards reality by trying to impose a 'winner' profile on readers that rarely captures people's imaginations for long because it is either impractical or unappealing.

Children and teachers were already familiar with the technique of philosophical enquiry and so the community of enquiry format was used to
discuss these questions and resolve them in ways the children thought
were *fair*. Obviously, the ways that some solutions were fair or not fair
had to be explored. The community of enquiry, with its emphasis on
respect, collaboration and reasoning, was ideal for this purpose; it helped
children to manage disagreement.

Carol Oliver found the whole experience to be a very powerful one
for children throughout the school. She noticed that children were able
to discuss, in mature ways, what qualities good representatives would
require: 'When children came to choose representatives for the council, they really looked for the qualities that had been discussed – they
didn't just vote for the most popular children in the class.' She also
noticed that the chosen children, often quiet but thoughtful, grew in
self-esteem and came to see their listening and reasoning skills as a
valued part of school life. They became examples for other children in
applying positive dispositions and skills.

Carol believes that staff at the school now realise that children can
handle difficult discussions and decision-making responsibilities:

'Members of staff have been impressed by the way children have not only been
able to question things but also to question things in the right manner – as if they
really want to understand and contribute if they can. This is all the more impres-
sive given some of the challenging children we have in the school. And it has
made us question some of our own assumptions, based on children's backgrounds,
about the levels of thinking they can achieve.'

The school council now meets regularly and N-RAIS consultants have
coached pupil representatives in the roles and skills required of them
during council meetings, such as 'recorders' and 'chairs'. The pupils
have settled on a model that uses an issues suggestion box in every
classroom. The whole class will prioritise the issues and send questions to the council about ones they find most important. The council
will go through the same process of prioritisation and send questions

back to the classes. The process is inclusive because it involves all children in discussion. So, for example, when one class suggested buying a climbing frame with the £1,000 available, the school council discussed the suggestion and realised that, with 300 pupils and only ten spaces on the climbing frame, each pupil would only be able to use it once a month. They passed this observation back to the class for further discussion along with other suggestions. The process obviously exercises sophisticated thinking skills, such as prioritising and imagining consequences as well as dispositions such as imagination, collaboration and dialogue.

At Tyndale Middle School, N-RAIS has taken the coaching of class representatives a stage further. Every pupil member of the council has been trained, over a period of two full days, to lead a classroom community of enquiry. Demanding challenges are tackled, such as facilitating discussion, encouraging others to speak, handling disagreement, keeping the discussion to the point and recording points raised. These young facilitators need a lot of encouragement and this comes mostly from the faith adults place in them and the careful preparation they receive through intensive coaching.

In Berwick, some 'partnerships' or networks of schools invite pupil representatives from each school to present an issue to them in the form of an enquiry on a question of importance to pupils. Local politicians, teachers and school managers attend the meetings and gain an insight into children's thinking on issues such as school bullying and the local response to the tsunami disaster.

Encouraging self-belief in the community

N-RAIS consultants have developed a course called *Encouraging Self-belief* that they offer to parents, teachers and community workers. One aim of the N-RAIS project is to have a positive effect on the whole community. In this course, N-RAIS consultants work directly with people who are responsible for encouraging others. N-RAIS advertises the course through educational or community networks and offers it to parents and teachers in all schools who work with them in any way. The purpose of the course is to help people encourage themselves.

Encouraging Self-belief begins with an open discussion amongst participants about the situations where they feel confident and those where they lack confidence. With sensitive guidance, this leads into further discussions about problems they may have in learning new things, seeing through goals or keeping positive in difficult circumstances.

The consultants introduce ideas about how words and images can affect emotions and motivation. Like sports coaches, they encourage positive self-talk. So, for example, people in the groups might tell themselves any of the following negative things:

- 'I've got no will power. I mean to read to my children but just can't face it; I feel too tired.'
- 'I don't agree with what is happening at work right now but I'm not confident enough to speak up and say what I think.'
- 'I want my children to help around the house more but I'm put off by the thought of all the hassle. I'm just a useless parent I guess.'
- 'I want to take a new course but I don't think I'm up to it. Maybe I'm not very bright.'

This kind of negative internal dialogue is obviously destructive but how can it be changed? Some ideas for group members to try out are:

- Try imagining how you feel when you achieve your goal. Try to really feel it.
- Focus on your strengths and assets. What resources do you have for tackling new challenges? How have they helped you to manage in the past?
- Create a picture in your minds of achieving what you want.
- Try talking to yourself in a positive way and see what difference it makes to your actions.
- Talk about the future as if it is already a reality: 'I am feeling loving because I'm reading with my child.'
- Try to reframe questions from being rhetorical and destructive into ones that pose a problem to be tackled: 'How will I find time to read to my child twice a week?' rather than 'why am I so useless?'

In Berwick, some 'partnerships' or networks of schools invite pupil representatives from each school to present an issue to them in the form of an enquiry on a question of importance to pupils. Local politicians, teachers and school managers attend the meetings and gain an insight into children's thinking on issues such as school bullying and the local response to the tsunami disaster.

- Think of a time when you were confident and thrilled at achieving a goal. Can you remember the sorts of things you said to yourself or anything about where it happened? Can you use an image of that as an anchor to lead you to more positive feelings in adversity?
- Distance yourself from your own negative voice. When you hear it, try to imagine it speaking in the voice of Micky Mouse. Does it sound so convincing?

These ideas are presented as possible strategies that could make a difference. Participants are invited to try them out and report back. The discussion continues. The strategies of visualization, anchoring and positive self-talk are familiar terms in the literature of Neuro-Linguistic Programming (NLP) – an approach to achieving personal goals by deliberately using key words, images and feelings to change behaviours (literally to reprogramme the brain). But N-RAIS consultants use these strategies as aids to the *art* of coaching and encouragement rather than as sure-fire solutions with *scientific* validity (real or imagined). There is no attempt to force a 'winner profile' onto people. The important thing is that the group becomes a mini-culture of encouragement.

People trust that others can achieve their goals and group members keep talking about what helps and what doesn't. That, in itself, is a powerful context for change. The specific strategies provide some practical starting points and complement the kinds of principles of effective encouragement outlined by Dinkmeyer, Dreikurs and others[29] that we summarise below:

1. Show faith in each person's basic abilities. Show faith in people as they are, not in how they could be.
2. Recognise and focus on strengths and assets.
3. Help people to define and achieve goals.
4. Use people's interests and aspirations to energise their development.
5. Be aware of people's feelings and the meanings they make out of their experiences. Ask questions, listen and try to understand.
6. Model the re-framing of problems and pessimistic thinking to energise effort.

7. Engineer opportunities for successful achievement.
8. Be pleased with efforts and contributions.
9. Promote the idea that it is good to try – failure is no crime and is the inevitable prerequisite of eventual success.

Deciding on particular goals is an important part of the *Encouraging Self-belief* course. N-RAIS consultants encourage people to think widely about areas of their lives such as career, family and friends, leisure and recreation, personal relationships, health and fitness and so on. Choosing a goal in any of these areas and pursuing it, with encouragement from others, is an experience many people find rewarding. Simply writing down a goal and committing to it with people who support you is a powerful stimulus to change.

Many teachers and community workers who have undertaken the course report that they feel more confident as a result of the coaching process. It is common for them to say they feel more able to present their ideas to work meetings or to persevere in the face of difficulties – in other words, to resist discouragement.

Parents have been able to reflect on their own successes and disappointments in education and on their current goals and aspirations. The courses have raised awareness about the importance of encouragement for themselves and their children. One group of mothers suffering from post-natal depression gained a lot from the course. Some typically positive reports from several participants were:

- 'I now like myself. It's nice to know you are not out there alone. I am now a very positive person. Goal setting is now a major part in my life. I am now planning to work towards a nursing degree.'
- 'The course has been one of the best things I have done for myself. It has helped change my life for the better. I now have a greater sense of self-worth and excitement about the future.'
- 'It has made me feel I am not alone but, most of all, that I can change the way I think. It helped me get over feeling panicky about going to the wedding of a friend I haven't seen for ten years. I'm now excited about going.'

Recently, N-RAIS consultants have begun a similar course with teenage parents. Goal setting, visualizing future achievements and positive self-talk have been, once again, the main strategies. The following statements reflect the aspirations of the teenagers to become more independent at home and more confident at work.

- 'I am really proud to be driving myself around in my own car by summer next year and I am happy to be more independent now.'
- 'By Easter next year I am talking confidently to professionals on the phone at work.'
- 'I am so excited to be sitting in my own home by Easter next year.'
- 'By summer next year I am really pleased and proud to be sitting in my newly-decorated house which looks warm and inviting.'

'Supporting your child's learning': A course for parents.

The N-RAIS team has developed another course for parents on how to support their children's learning. It starts with reflection on their own experiences of learning and being parents. Then it coaches them in the use of strategies for encouraging their children using principles such as those listed overleaf. Parents are invited to draw on their own experiences of times when they felt encouraged or discouraged and to identify the reasons why. They are coached to help children deal with stress, to persevere, to be adventurous, to be curious and to try out new things. All parents want to encourage their children but many haven't had an opportunity to discuss what that means in practice or how to overcome the difficulties that inevitably arise because of established personalities, habits or routines. The N-RAIS course provides such an opportunity. One parent's comments sum up the experience:

'My daughter's learning ability is much the same as my own at her age. She has a slow pace, needs time to think and her confidence is not brilliant. I feel for her problems one hundred per cent. I found the course very enlightening and the strategies which we were given have helped me to help her in a much more stress-free way.'

PRINCIPLES OF EFFECTIVE ENCOURAGEMENT

Show faith in each person's basic abilities. Show faith in people as they are, not in how they could be.

Recognise and focus on strengths and assets.

Help people to define and achieve goals.

Use people's interests and aspirations to energise their development.

Be aware of people's feelings and the meanings they make out of their experiences. Ask questions, listen and try to understand.

Model the re-framing of problems and pessimistic thinking to energise effort.

Engineer opportunities for successful achievement.

Be pleased with efforts and contributions.

Promote the idea that it is good to try – failure is no crime and is the inevitable prerequisite of eventual success.

A virtuous circle of encouragement

The N-RAIS team is expanding its range of clients through contacts with local professional and voluntary groups working in the community. The course with teenage parents, for example, arose because a group of social workers volunteered for the *Encouraging Self-belief* course, liked it, and thought it would benefit the teenagers. Thus, through educational and community networks, N-RAIS strives to develop a cycle of encouragement in homes, schools and communities. The encouragement is targeted towards developing positive dispositions, skills and strategies. It is a radical and ambitious goal. N-RAIS has shown that many of the techniques of coaching can work in educational and community settings – particularly when people are coached not only to help themselves but also to help others.

Summary

Teaching inevitably involves an element of coaching but a more intensive or structured use of coaching techniques by teachers can often help students who are discouraged in some area of learning or who need extra help to develop a personal resource or fulfil a role. Coaching can also help with social activities such as collaborating on intellectual and physical challenges. Social competencies support individual ones and vice versa.

In school situations where there is a wide variety of values, abilities and goals, coaching should be accompanied by opportunities for dialogue between teachers and pupils. Philosophical enquiry is a good vehicle for this kind of dialogue.

4

Teaching Thinking Skills

In previous chapters, we described how the Radical Encouragement approach aims to develop people's resources for learning in the pursuit of positive goals. In this chapter, we discuss the contribution that teaching for 'thinking skills' can play in developing the resources of learners by acknowledging the arguments against the concepts of thinking skills and responding to them. We summarise the strategies that N-RAIS consultants advocate for teaching thinking skills and stress their belief that such strategies are most effective when used to provide stimulus and support for learning dialogues in which key concepts for thinking can be introduced, practised and transferred to other contexts.

MOST PEOPLE who now advocate the teaching of thinking skills see it as obvious that pupils should possess the kinds of intellectual and emotional resources that help them rise to challenges both in and out of school. The term 'skill' is applied to a wide range of intellectual behaviours that demonstrate the use of resources, including:

•   The effective use of 'tools' to help organise one's thinking. Examples include Venn diagrams (for categorising) and 'fishbone' diagrams for listing causes.[30]

- Using 'self-talk' to lessen the chances of making mistakes. Examples include De Bono's well-known acronym, CAF: *Consider All Factors.*[31]
- The ability to make certain kinds of 'moves' either in dialogue or in one's thinking. Examples include looking for examples or counter-examples of a principle, speculating and checking, and connecting reasons to conclusions in an orderly way.
- Using strategies to guide oneself through a challenge. Examples include problem-solving formulae and strings of appropriate questions.
- A facility with a 'thinking vocabulary' of concept words such as category, distinction, cause and so on.
- Displaying dispositions such as curiosity and persistence when faced with intellectual challenges.

In each case, the concept of 'skill' is appropriate in the sense that it describes a behaviour, gained by experience, that is appropriate, deliberate and effective. Advocates of thinking skills also tend to assume that such behaviours can transfer across subject boundaries. In other words, the same dispositions, strategies, moves, vocabulary, tools and self-talk will help with many kinds of challenges across the curriculum and beyond.

Controversy over thinking skills

Although the idea of teaching thinking skills is popular, it remains a controversial one. Some of the arguments against teaching thinking skills seem to highlight problems with commonly-held but naive beliefs. Engaging with these arguments can, in our view, help develop an effective practice of teaching thinking skills.

There are two main arguments against the idea that general thinking skills can be taught. The first claims that there is little good evidence that teaching thinking skills makes an impact in schools. The second claims that thinking is so bound up with content knowledge that it cannot be taught separately as something 'general' apart from content. Both of these arguments are based on a now out-of-date view of thinking skills as abstract 'cognitive structures'.

Argument from evidence of 'transfer'

The movement of skills learnt in one context to applications of those skills in other contexts is called 'transfer'. Thinking skills programmes seek to teach skills that transfer to a wide range of other contexts. Some opponents of thinking skills claim that this transfer has not been demonstrated.

However, there is now some good statistical evidence that thinking skills programmes can transfer. For example, some have been shown to be correlated with greater achievement in exams in a range of subject areas.[32] At the same time, research suggests that some approaches succeed where others fail. One large study of a range of thinking-skills programmes found those which succeeded best in their general impact on educational achievement were ones that included work on emotions and students' self-image as learners.[33] This would seem to support the Radical Encouragement approach of strengthening learners' self-stories through developing their intellectual and emotional resources.

The other important conclusion that emerges from these studies is that transfer is only likely when groups of students talk together and teachers explicitly show pupils how a strategy taught in one context can be applied in another. This is sometimes referred to in thinking skills literature as 'bridging'. The fact that transfer only seems to occur when there is bridging and talk implies that thinking skills are not found in 'cognitive structures', as previously argued in some thinking skills literature, but in resources gained through dialogue and encouragement.

Cognitive structures and problem-solving formulae

It is often argued that if children are taught how to solve problems in one area they will develop general 'cognitive structures' that enable them to solve logically similar problems in other areas. This claim is found in many logic and problem-solving programmes. Yet the evidence is that this approach does not work or, at least, does not work in the way that it was assumed to do. For example, the programming lan-

One large study of a range of thinking-skills programmes found that those that succeeded best in their general impact on educational achievement were ones that included work on emotions and students' self-image as learners. This would seem to support the Radical Encouragement approach of strengthening learners' self-stories through developing their intellectual and emotional resources.

guage, LOGO, has been taught for a long time in UK schools and throughout the world. It is the language that is used to programme 'roamers' or 'turtles' as part of primary maths. Part of its attraction to educators has been the claim that learning LOGO can improve thinking generally because it requires logical thinking.

The research findings, however, show that students can become better at programming in LOGO without any evidence of an impact on their thinking and learning outside the LOGO environment. Even when the logical structure of a problem that they can solve in LOGO is the same as a problem presented in different terms in mathematics, science or history, students cannot transfer their skills in LOGO to other contexts.[34]

There is a similar lack of supporting evidence for the sort of general problem-solving formulae that can be used in any subject area. Extensive research over many years has failed to find general laws or formulae for good problem-solving. In every subject, thinking and content knowledge have been found to be hard to disentangle.

Thinking is always bound up with the content matter of what is thought about. We have already mentioned the usefulness of having a general concept of *feeding forward* and *feeding back*[35] – noticing, imagining, planning, trying out, checking and adjusting. Most problem-solving formulae are built around this two-fold process.[36] Implementing the process in different subject areas, however, will require some experience of the most fruitful things to try out, the ability to carry out what must be done and suitable criteria for checking on results.

It may well be true that there are no universal laws or formulae behind good thinking, applicable to any situation, of the kind that could be written down and used to programme a computer. However, it does not follow from this that there are no general thinking skills.

Perhaps the mistake that has been made in the past has been to think about thinking in too abstract a way on the model of logic, flow charts and computer programmes. Experience teaches that good thinking is seldom simply a matter of following explicit and rigid rules. It also involves our knowledge, institutions, emotions and imaginations. Those who deny the existence of general thinking skills may well be looking for them in the wrong place. It is quite possible that there are no abstract 'cognitive structures' or general problem-solving formulae that apply to every subject area, much less to every area of life. Yet we can still argue that there are general thinking skills – if we interpret 'skills' as fruitful behaviours drawing on resources one has at one's disposal. These resources are appropriated through dialogue, practice and encouragement.

There are many resources, including dispositions, skills, strategies and tools, that are general to a range of thinking contexts. Language is perhaps the most general of all tools that help thinking. Skill in using language to think conceptually, clarify and solve problems is perhaps the most general thinking skill of all. There is good evidence that this general ability to use language (including sign systems like number, music and graphics) can be acquired through education. Indeed, some have claimed that being able to use language to think conceptually is essentially what it means to be an educated person.

The importance, across a range of subject areas, of using language as a tool for thinking could explain why research on LOGO and other thinking skills programmes has consistently shown the worth of dialogue and shared enquiry. It is through these that students can first hear, use and practise key concepts and moves that later become their own tools for thinking. These resources interact with background knowledge and a task to generate cycles of feeding forward and feeding back, thus directing learners' efforts to enquire, understand or create meaning in fruitful ways.

Why teach thinking skills?

We have argued that the skills of general conceptual thinking are developed with the acquisition of subject knowledge and vice versa. The two enhance each other. Yet the focus of most teaching is the acquisition of content. The teaching of thinking skills often remains incidental. It is not normally planned or given time during the course of the school day, even though many teachers would agree that one of the most important aims of education should be to help students become independent thinkers and learners. In recent initiatives, however, the

EXAMPLES OF RESOURCES AS THINKING SKILLS
A REMINDER

The effective use of 'tools' to help organise one's thinking. Examples include Venn diagrams (for categorising) and 'fishbone' diagrams for listing causes.

Using 'self-talk' to lessen the chances of making mistakes. Examples include De Bono's well-known acronym, CAF: *Consider All Factors*.

The ability to make certain kinds of 'moves' either in dialogue or in one's thinking. Examples include looking for examples or counter-examples of a principle, speculating and checking, and connecting reasons to conclusions in an orderly way.

Using strategies to guide oneself through a challenge. Examples include problem-solving formulae and strings of appropriate questions.

A facility with a 'thinking vocabulary' of concept words such as category, distinction, cause and so on.

Displaying dispositions such as curiosity and persistence when faced with intellectual challenges.

We argue that these kinds of resources can be used flexibly in many contexts. They interact with background knowledge and a task and they develop general conceptual thinking.

UK Department for Education and Skills (DfES) appears to have accepted the importance of teaching thinking. Among the strategies recommended to secondary schools, for example, we read that:

> 'Teaching thinking involves the creation of challenging learning experiences which call for high-level thinking, such as the development of the skills listed in the National Curriculum Orders for England under the five headings of information processing, reasoning, enquiry, creative thinking and evaluation. The main focus for teaching thinking is on developing pupils' ability as learners. Pupils need to consider not only what has been learned but also how it has been learned so that they can transfer these skills more readily to other areas and subjects. Without the right words, thinking and learning are difficult to discuss so teachers need to develop a 'thinking' vocabulary for pupils to use. The ultimate aim is for pupils to become independent thinkers, capable of planning for, checking and reflecting on their thinking across different types of tasks.' [37]

This clearly signals a shift towards the kind of teaching and learning that will equip students with the resources they need to be able to think effectively in a range of contexts. The same government strategy document goes on to list the kinds of things that teachers should do in order to develop the thinking skills of students. This list is worth quoting because it summarises many features of the approach to teaching thinking skills taken by the N-RAIS project.

- Setting challenging tasks that encourage pupils to strive to think through a problem or issue which may have no single correct answer.
- Planning for learning objectives which encourage pupils to gain an understanding of the patterns of thinking and principal concepts in each subject.
- Encouraging pupils to use and build on what they already know in order to make sense of new information.
- Planning for pupils to 'think together' through collaborative talk and active listening.

- Intervening, when necessary, by asking questions which support or extend pupils' thinking.
- Using the plenary session to check learning against objectives and to debrief pupils on both their solutions to the task and their strategies for carrying it out.
- Helping pupils to make connections between the thinking involved in the task and other contexts in order to encourage transfer of knowledge and skills.[38]

It is one thing for the government to exhort teachers to teach for thinking and to offer principles to guide them, it is quite another to change the way that teaching is done. It may be, for example, that teachers use recommended strategies and tasks without really being clear about what they should be working towards (*ie* the development of resources that students can use independently). Sometimes, too, teachers feel discouraged when new initiatives are introduced in an educational culture which is, in general, coercive.

Yet, time and again, the Northumberland teachers we interviewed told us that N-RAIS had helped them transform their practice, sometimes using strategies approved by government documents and sometimes using others. The N-RAIS approach is one of encouragement and dialogue.

A whole-school approach

When schools were contacted by the N-RAIS team, all the teaching staff, assistants and governors were invited for an initial session where they were told about the support that N-RAIS could offer and shown some of the possible techniques, including teaching strategies, challenges, philosophical enquiry and coaching, that we describe in detail in other chapters of this book. After these tasters, staff were invited to make a positive choice about where to start. The purpose of this whole-school approach was that all staff would share the same language of thinking skills and the same goal of empowering pupils. *Philosophy for Children*, for example, develops children's curiosity and their ability to ask good questions. When staff in a school are committed to furthering these dispositions and skills, they will give pupils opportunities to develop their questioning in all areas of school life. In secondary schools, particular departments often took the lead in adopting agreed aims and strategies.

Thinking vocabulary

Once staff agree on a starting point, they will need to discuss how to help learners develop resources to use independently. Strategies for thinking skills will be effective to the extent that they enhance learners' conceptual thinking.

Each subject has its particular 'big concepts' but many important concepts describing relationships are shared across a range of subjects. The critic and educationalist, I. A. Richards, argued that effective thinking depended on facility with a number of key concepts. He listed words that embodied these concepts and described them as the most important words in the language for two reasons:

1. They cover the ideas we can least avoid using – those which are concerned in all that we do as thinking begins.
2. They are words we are forced to use in explaining other words because it is in terms of the ideas they cover that the meanings of other words must be given.[39]

Steve Williams has arranged some of the key words from Richards' list, along with some additions, into families of relationships.

Pause for thought: Consider your teaching and the pupils you teach.

- Which of the following families of words are the key ones for thinking about relationships and making meaning in your lessons?
- Are some families of relationships more important to some subjects than others?
- Do some new words, or families of words, need to be added?

Families of concepts
describing relationships

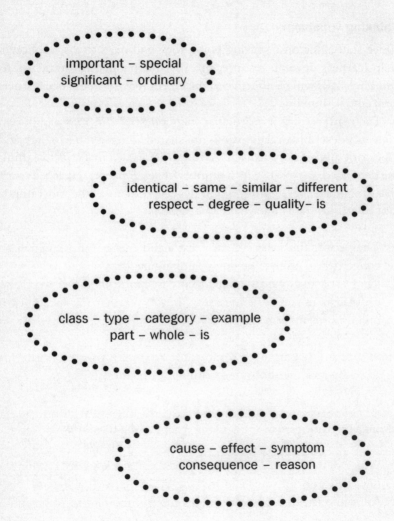

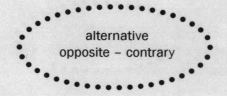

alternative
opposite – contrary

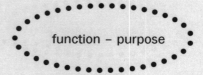

function – purpose

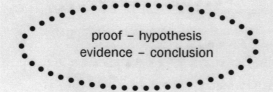

proof – hypothesis
evidence – conclusion

at the same time
before – after
always

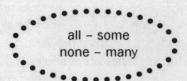

all – some
none – many

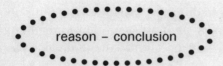

reason – conclusion

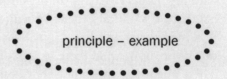

principle – example

part – whole
multiple – single
complete – incomplete

Activities that lead to the mobilisation of these relational families of concepts in classroom discussions will be particularly valuable for developing thinking. However, teachers should also pause to discuss with students what jobs the concept words do in each context where they arise. Words like this can't be defined easily. Their value lies in their flexibility. One has to understand them by using them and discussing their use. So, for example, the activity of comparing will mobilise concept-words like same, different, similar, degree, quality, class, copy, significant and so on. To compare is an essential strategy for all learning and understanding. To compare thoroughly we must consider the qualities and degrees of similarity and difference. We must also think about which similarities and differences are most significant to the purpose of our enquiry. The following sentences demonstrate the complexity of the word 'same':

- Hitler and Stalin were the same. They were both tyrants.
- Cloning means remaking an organism to be the same as the original with an identical genetic structure.
- A cloned sheep and the original sheep are not the same sheep – otherwise, how could there be two of them?
- These poems are the same. They both express feelings of lost love.

If we say that Hitler and Stalin were the same kinds of leaders (tyrants), are we saying that they share this quality? Is the degree of tyranny they showed different from that of other leaders one could describe as 'tyrannous'? We could also enquire into the ways that Hitler and Stalin were different. After all, the tyrants' differences might be equally or more significant than their similarities. Discussions exploring these types of questions develop our understanding of essential concept words for thinking. The value of such discussions is not limited to the particular subjects from which they arise. They echo across subjects, enhancing our abilities to think flexibly and deeply about whatever we encounter.

In science, for example, students may learn about the extraction of aluminium by electrolysis. They may commit to memory the fact that, during the extraction process, positively-charged ions gain electrons at the negative electrode. They may have little understanding of what ions and electrons are, nor any inclination to improve their understanding by asking the teacher. However, an experienced learner will start to ask questions to build a framework of understanding: 'What is the difference between ions and electrons? How are they the same and how do they differ? Is an electron part of an ion or are they both part of something else? How do they relate to atoms? What are their functions?' These questions are rooted in the families of relational concepts which apply to all subjects.

Learners need to become expert in using the families of concepts through discussion across the curriculum in all the forms of thinking, talking and writing that people use to make meaning, including:

- arguments
- statements
- questions
- analogies
- metaphors
- stories
- essays
- diagrams

The web of concepts

Everyday language often relates closely to a particular physical or social context. A mechanic might ask his workmate to 'pass the wrench', for example, without the need for any complicated thinking. Conceptual language, on the other hand, draws us inevitably into general thinking because concepts, by their nature, relate more to other concepts than to actions in an immediate physical or social context. The skill of thinking conceptually in one area is similar in some ways to the skill of thinking conceptually in another area. The general thinking skill involved here is not best described as a 'cognitive structure', it is the ability to use language to think conceptually and flexibly. Vygotsky sees the development of conceptual thinking as one of the main functions of schooling:[40]

'Concepts do not lie in a child's mind like peas in a pod, without any bonds between them. If that were the case, no intellectual operation requiring coordination would be possible, nor would any general conception of the world … one must turn from a study of concepts as isolated entities to a study of the 'fabric' made of concepts. The teacher's role is to mediate concepts to develop the web of meaning … Once a new structure has been incorporated into his thinking – usually through school – it spreads to the older concepts as they are drawn into the intellectual operations …'

Visual tools

Visual 'tools' for thinking, such as Venn diagrams and MindMaps™, are immensely useful for helping us to think conceptually. There are several reasons for this:

* Many important concepts are expressed through metaphors of space or movement. Our concepts of category and class, for example, are connected to the image of a container (a bounded region in space). We talk about something being *in* a certain category. A Venn diagram with its graphic borders helps us to clarify the concept of 'category' because we literally place an object *in* a space representing the category.
* Diagrams help us to see relationships systematically, all at once and in a pattern. They hold our thinking steady and accessible while we seek out further connections and reflect on the ones we have already charted. In this way, diagrams react with our thinking, speaking and writing to stimulate, direct and organise our ideas.

Many of the techniques for teaching thinking skills recommended in the various government strategies in England and Wales depend on visual tools or on arranging material in patterns to make relationships clear. However, the success with which these techniques will improve pupils' thinking will depend on how well they help students internalise the concepts they represent. This is illustrated on the following pages by listing some common tools and exploring their links with families of concepts.

MindMaps™ (and *model maps*) represent categories and associations in a web-like diagram radiating from a central point.[41]

Families of concepts possibly mobilised by using MindMaps™ include:
- class, type, category, example, part, whole, is
- principle, example
- part, whole, multiple, single, complete, incomplete
- cause, effect, symptom, consequence, reason
- function, purpose
- proof, hypothesis, evidence, conclusion
- reason, conclusion

Odd One Out is a task set to stimulate thinking about similarities and differences between three or more items using diagrammatic representation. After similarities and differences have been established, significance is discussed using the prompt: 'Find the odd one out'. This prompts discussion about which differences and similarities are most important.[42]

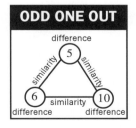

Families of concepts possibly mobilised by using Odd One Out include:
- identical, same, similar, different, respect, degree, quality, is
- reason, conclusion
- important, special, significant, ordinary
- class, type, category, example, part, whole, is
- principle, example

Affinity diagrams (used as the basis of *Mysteries*).[43] This is an arrange-ment of items under headings of affinity established through discus-sion. In the case of *Mysteries,* a question is presented (often about why something happened). Cards with statements written on them are given to students who arrange them under headings of their own devising. Typical headings might be: not causes, most likely causes, least likely causes, causes to do with humans, causes to do with the environment. The flexibility in the task allows students to discuss, analyse and change their minds.

Families of concepts possibly mobilised by using Affinity diagrams and/or Mys-teries include:

- class, type, category, example, part, whole, is
- cause, effect, symptom, consequence, reason
- alternative, opposite, contrary
- reason, conclusion
- important, special, significant, ordinary
- proof, hypothesis, evidence, conclusion

Targets. Ideas or items are arranged in concentric circles to indicate importance or degrees of affinity. They also could be used, for example, to apply criteria for judgement. Three concentric circles could represent three criteria for judgement. Placing an item in the outer ring would indicate that it meets one criteria. A bulls-eye indicates that all three criteria have been met.

Families of concepts possibly mobilised by Affinity diagrams or mysteries include:
- class, type, category, example, part, whole, is
- reason, conclusion
- important, special, significant, ordinary
- part, whole, multiple, single, complete, incomplete

Fortune lines.[44] These are chronological representations of an event (like timelines) but with a vertical axis showing a scale of good or bad fortune. They could be applied to a story like Little Red Riding Hood or a period in a nation's history. They stimulate discussion of sequences (what happened before and after?), significance (what were the important events?) and judgement supported by reasons (who was the event good for and why?)

Families of concepts possibly mobilised by Fortune lines include:
- at the same time, before, after, always
- reason, conclusion
- important, special, significant, ordinary
- proof, hypothesis, evidence, conclusion

Diamond ranking. An arrangement showing importance or significance, with most space in the middle and least space at the top and bottom. Ranking tasks could obviously use other shapes such as pyramids, inverted pyramids or simple lists.

Families of concepts possibly mobilised by Diamond ranking include:
- reason, conclusion
- important, special, significant, ordinary
- proof, hypothesis, evidence, conclusion
- identical, same, similar, different, respect, degree, quality, is

Progression

It should be clear that these kinds of visual tools and strategies for teachers to use in lessons will engage students and teachers in dialogue about important concepts. They will graphically represent those concepts to learners and may help them to transfer the concepts to new situations.[45] However, when teachers think about how to develop pupils' thinking in their lessons, their planning will not so much involve them in devising more and harder tasks like *Odd One Out,* but rather in working towards students coming up independently with the same questions prompted by the diagrams. Effective learners will generate questions like: *What is similar? What is different? What is the most significant? Is this part of a category of things I should be looking out for? What should I do first? What comes next?* Effective learners will also know when they need to use visual tools and when they don't.

If visual tools are used simply to vary classroom activities, then they will not serve to develop learners' thinking across the curriculum. It is a mistake to believe that by using a visual tool or basing an activity around one, teachers will improve their pupils' thinking skills through the exercise of 'mental muscles' or the development of 'cognitive structures'.

For this reason, N-RAIS consultants stress the importance of dialogue about the relationship between visual tools and concepts. They will encourage talk about appropriate opportunities to use the tools and concepts across the curriculum. They will also discuss how students have handled tasks and what strategies they could adapt to use in other contexts. They call these reflective processes *thinking about thinking* and sometimes *debriefing*.[46]

Thinking about thinking and debriefing

We know from research studies that transfer of thinking skills is only likely when groups of students talk together about how a strategy used in one context can be applied in another. We have also identified 'skills' as a range of intellectual behaviours that reveal resources including: effective use of tools for thinking, application of a variety of discussion moves, positive self-talk, facility with concepts and language and positive dispositions. Teachers will talk to pupils about these things during and after any session which aims to develop their thinking skills. N-RAIS consultants refer to these dialogues as *thinking about thinking* or *debriefing*. There is some overlap here with the term 'metacognition', used in many books about thinking skills. It is important to note that dialogue can be about a range of aspects of thinking, as illustrated in the diagram on the following page. It should not be narrowed down to one aspect, such as what learners found difficult and how they tried to overcome the difficulty.

If visual tools are used simply to vary classroom activities, then they will not serve to develop learners' thinking across the curriculum. It is a mistake to believe that by using a visual tool or basing an activity around one, teachers will improve their pupils' thinking skills through the exercise of 'mental muscles' or the development of 'cognitive structures'.

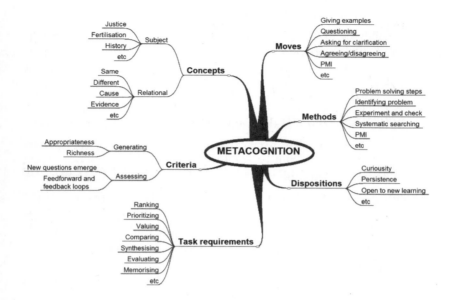

Problem-solving strategies and thinking about thinking

We have argued that there are no universal strategies that work the same way in every context. We can all benefit from strategic thinking and often use a strategy in more than one context if we are able to think flexibly or create analogies. Let's look at an example. Imagine an inter-action between a mother and her young son, who has lost his teddy bear.[47]

The mother asks some questions: 'Did you leave him in your bed-room? Did you take him into the garden? Did you give him some food in the kitchen?' The child replies: 'Not in garden ... I gave teddy some food... in the kitchen'. Here, the mother uses questions to organise the retrieval of fragments of information from the child's memory in or-der to narrow the search. The child does not know how to organise the information but he does have the information needed to find the teddy bear. Through collaboration, mother and son produce a satisfactory solution. As the child grows older, he will learn to use the same kind of questions to look for lost items.

What should we call the mother's helpful actions? She has surely demonstrated a strategy for thinking (a variation of *feedforward* and *feedback*) and she has provided her son with a resource for finding things. The possession of relevant information is, on its own, not enough for good thinking. But will this strategy help in other contexts? In science, for example, the process of considering alternative hypotheses while searching for the truth is different from considering alternative locations for a lost teddy bear.

However, it would not be hard to imagine science teachers using the mother's questioning strategy as an analogy for judging between alternative hypotheses in science, particularly if their pupils found more abstract explanations of scientific method difficult to understand. What are the differences between the two kinds of thinking? In science, a comparison of alternative hypotheses does not necessarily release information we already have; it may point us towards information we need to find out through experiment. This kind of articulation and comparison of thinking strategies is a helpful process for students, particularly when it is flexible and analogical. It is a form of *thinking about thinking*.

Many of the strategies developed by Edward De Bono[48] that are used in schools and businesses are designed to remind people not to rush to conclusions before considering alternatives. So, for example, his CAF strategy reminds people to *Consider All Factors*; his PMI (*Plus, Minus, Interesting*) strategy prompts us not to pass judgements too quickly on issues before looking at alternative viewpoints. A strategy like CAF can be useful in many contexts provided teachers discuss with pupils what the concept of 'factor' means in each context. What, for example, would be the factors one needs to consider in a science experiment and how would they differ from those one would look for when interpreting a poem? These discussions not only help learners develop flexible strategies, they also learn about the essential principles that underpin each subject.

Dispositions, tools, strategies and concepts

We have seen that many personal resources – including dispositions, strategies and tools – are general to a range of thinking contexts. Language is the most general of all tools that help thinking. Skill in using language is perhaps the most general thinking skill of all. This could explain why research on LOGO and other thinking-skills programmes shows the importance of promoting discussion and shared enquiry. It is in dialogues that students can first use and practise key concept words, arguments and strategies, which can then become general tools for thinking in a range of other contexts. That is why N-RAIS consultants prioritise three key elements of teaching thinking skills:

1. Using appropriate tools to stimulate conceptual thinking.
2. Using dialogue about general concepts for thinking and progression towards students internalising these concepts.
3. Thinking about thinking and debriefing in order to transfer skills across the curriculum.

Summary

The concept of 'thinking skills' is a controversial one. We think of a 'skill' as a behaviour, gained by experience, that is appropriate, deliberate and effective, rather than a cognitive structure in the mind. General thinking skills will help learners achieve success in intellectual challenges both in and out of school. However, skills gained in one context will only transfer to others if there is dialogue, particularly about underlying concepts and differences in the applications of strategies to each context. This accounts for the emphasis that N-RAIS consultants place on discussion, thinking about thinking and debriefing.

5

Teachers Need Encouragement Too

In this chapter, Martin Renton, a teacher at Amble Middle School until 2005,
writes about his experiences of working with the N-RAIS team. He argues that
encouragement is not only important for learners, it is essential for teachers too. He
describes how using strategies recommended by the N-RAIS team made his job
more intellectually stimulating.

I HAVE TO ADMIT that when the head told us that he had booked an *N-RAIS Day*, I was not particularly thrilled by the prospect of another set of consultants coming into school to tell us how to become better teachers. But I was to be proved wrong in my concerns because the continuing effects of the *N-RAIS Day* have changed my approach in the classroom and have completely altered my attitude to professional development.

What I wanted from professional development

Making changes in the classroom is not an easy thing to do, particularly if you feel that the way you teach is already effective. But a good teacher is a flexible, adaptable teacher. Even if making changes appears daunting, it is worth making mistakes and discovering new approaches in order to branch out, challenge yourself, enjoy your job and avoid stagnation.

Teachers will not want to change unless there is a 'hook' – the spark that will fire their imaginations and enthuse them to develop their teaching practices. Once they have the desire to change, then support and expert advice is a bonus.

For me, the hook was my classroom ethos – my teaching style and the relationships between the pupils and between the pupils and myself. I wanted to develop a classroom ethos that fostered a network of open discussion. Focusing on the purpose behind the change was vital to the support I received from N-RAIS.

The N-RAIS approach. How it worked for me

To begin with, the N-RAIS partnership presented an *N-RAIS Day*: a demonstration of strategies to develop thinking skills and positive dispositions. Staff gave a positive reception to the consultants because they weren't seen as a group of advisors telling teachers that their methods had been wrong for years. N-RAIS staff were actually going to teach in the school – and teach a *full* class for a *full* day! Staff could choose to attend the sessions that most interested them. This allowed us to take from the day what *we* felt was most relevant to our practice.

I had the opportunity to see two sessions, one using thinking skills strategies such as *Odd One Out*, the other a *Philosophy for Children* lesson. In both lessons, the trainers demonstrated the strategies whilst also dealing with classroom management and behaviour issues.

If a class teacher had needed to discipline the pupils on behalf of an N-RAIS consultant, the day would have been open to the criticism that good behaviour was a prerequisite for success and that the strategies might not be suitable for 'difficult' classes. But the N-RAIS consultants demonstrated that they were skilled teachers, not just people with ideas about what other teachers should do.

That fact that children responded well demonstrated the suitability of the strategies and supported the claim that they could play a role in improving pupils' behaviours and attitudes. The debrief at the end of the *N-RAIS Day* made it clear that any further individual professional development was optional. I found this more motivating than being instructed to make changes.

I explained to one of the trainers that I wished to develop a classroom ethos of talk and open relationships and felt that the thinking skills and *Philosophy for Children* sessions I'd seen that day might be appropriate in helping to achieve this. I was introduced to a second member of the team whose expertise and subject area matched mine.

This first meeting is vital if teachers are expected to opt in. Working with someone in your classroom for a number of weeks, having them observe your teaching style and inevitably making mistakes in front of them, requires someone who you can trust. You are in a professionally vulnerable position, so a good one-to-one relationship is crucial.

Finding the right person for the role – someone who provides encouragement, support, listening skills and, for me, a good sense of humour – makes the partnership successful. If we believe that good teaching takes place in a classroom ethos of support and positivity, then the same must apply in a professional context for teacher improvement. If the trainer wants the teacher to attempt new strategies in the classroom, then a constructive two-way flow of ideas and information is necessary.

Picture for a moment JRR Tolkein and CS Lewis drinking coffee in a smoke-filled café one afternoon. The conversation turns to the fictitious Middle Earth: an ordinary land that looks like any other. As they start to talk it grows, developing shires, fortresses, creatures and, of course, the Ring. The story develops into an epic trilogy and later becomes a box-office smash. The ideas and the enthusiasm came from Tolkein but his ideas expanded through his conversations with Lewis. Substitute the café for the school, Middle Earth for the classroom, the Ring for a circle of chairs and the box-office smash for 30 happy pupils, and you have the cycle that developed with N-RAIS.

By sharing ideas with an external agent, we sometimes clarify our own ideas, view something from a new perspective or find answers that had eluded us before. The development of a positive one-to-one relationship bred the trust, enthusiasm and motivation that helped me improve my classroom practice.

Making changes in the classroom

Knowing our brief, we set about planning some changes in a couple of after-school meetings. We designed an alternative approach to a humanities topic that I was already comfortable teaching. We used the learning objectives from the existing scheme of work as the basis for a series of lessons which required talking and thinking strategies. The purposes of the lessons stayed the same; the means by which they were achieved changed completely.

This wasn't new – I had tried a few thinking strategies before but had found the lessons lacking in focus. I realise now that this was the result of attempting the strategies without comprehending the philosophy behind them. So the purpose of the intervention became 'understanding the philosophy behind my classroom practice' and we began by looking at why we want children to 'think' in the first place.

By analysing some of the strands in the complex nature of our own classroom teaching, we can learn much about our approach to education and can interweave new ideas with existing practice.

During an examination of my own teaching, my N-RAIS guide, David, introduced the notion of debriefing. I had assumed this was just a fancy term for the plenary which was, itself, just a fancy term for tidying up before the bell rings. However, David's expert knowledge challenged my view, demonstrating that the debrief plays a vital role in the learning process by teasing out from the children *how* they had completed the tasks and how those skills can then be *transferred* to other contexts. The children have to think about thinking.

Together, we planned a lesson with an *Odd One Out* starter, followed by a card-sorting activity using diamond ranking in order to encourage focused talk in pairs. At the end of the lesson, we hoped to debrief the pupils on their strategies for categorising and ranking the cards, and on how they felt thinking strategies and paired talk had helped them achieve the learning objectives. They talked about their use of significant words for thinking such as *important, significant, similar* and *different.*

The first lesson

The topic of my lesson was 'changing technology in the home'. I placed three pictures of different household items on the board. 'Can anyone spot the odd one out?' I asked, with the smug satisfaction of a newly-converted, forward-thinking teacher. Then I braced myself, imagining a barrage of arms in the air as the pupils, keen to share their deep, philosophical points of view, engaged in enthusiastic class debate.

> Lengthy pause.
> Lengthy pause becomes uncomfortable.
> One hand slowly rises (*'Thank goodness for that!'*).
> 'Yes, Andrew ...'
> 'Can I go for my guitar lesson?'

And it was downhill from there. I panicked and started asking bizarre questions in an effort to sound like a 'thinking-skills teacher' (whatever they sound like), so the lesson lacked focus, the children didn't appear to be learning anything and my usual, relaxed style disappeared. Getting answers from the children became virtually impossible, and then I did something I hadn't done for years ... I went to my desk and referred to the lesson plan! My comfort zone was well and truly left behind.

Having exhausted the usefulness of the starter activity (in five minutes), I felt uncomfortable about the diamond-ranking task. The fact that there was someone watching me teaching badly made me feel even worse. I imagined David at the back of the room with a clipboard, furiously writing notes and putting enormous crosses on a checklist. I half-expected him to take over my lesson. I looked at him beseechingly.

He was standing at the side of the classroom, grinning like a Cheshire cat! He gave me a thumbs-up and winked! He wasn't flustered or concerned. On the pretence of borrowing a pencil from my desk, he quietly said: 'Remember that the children need to get used to working this way as well. Don't panic; just take your time. It won't be perfect straight away.'

On my own, I would have given up and reverted to my former safe and reliable practice. But thanks to David's encouragement, I explained the purpose of diamond ranking more clearly than I had the starter. The class discussed what would make successful paired talk and considered strategies for categorising the cards. Then I gave them some questions to consider for diamond ranking in pairs. David was right: as the children got used to it, they got better at it and as I got used to them working this way and could gauge their reactions to each task, my explanations improved. I began to relax and enjoy myself.

'Listen!' said David at one point. We were standing in the middle of the room, surrounded by children talking about changes in technology. Some were reading from cards, others giving opinions, and one pair was even arguing about the importance of the microwave oven over the television! There was the purposeful buzz of focused talk.

It is worth noting here that, despite a disappointing start, the children hadn't become silly or badly behaved and the lesson didn't fall into chaos – an experienced teacher won't suddenly lose good classroom management skills in one lesson. And the debrief? One minute before the end of the lesson, I asked the children to tidy their desks as quickly as possible before the bell rang. Oops!

Feeding back and planning together

Teachers are used to being observed in the classroom – from teacher-training to performance management and of course, OfSTED inspections. The feedback that follows these observations tends to be judgmental (however positively framed the criticism might be) and, perhaps because of this, teachers tend to approach observed lessons with a sense of paranoia and insecurity.

For this reason, David explained that our post-lesson discussion would be a debrief, just as that with the pupils. A key feature is to ask ourselves what we have learnt from the intervention and how we are going to change, improve or extend ideas for the next session. There were no judgmental terms used and David didn't lead the debriefing session. Together we focused on *our* ideas and *our* planning.

We did not discuss teaching skills or the personality of the teacher but rather the use of the thinking strategies and how to coax further talk for purpose from the children. In this way, the post-lesson debrief seemed non-judgemental and therefore non-threatening.

When we discussed the *Odd One Out* starter, we recognised that I had received little response from the children in class discussion. In a judgemental observation, that would have appeared in the 'weaknesses' box (unless there is a new 'well done for attempting something different' box), but David and I debated why the children might not have reacted as we expected and decided that the pupils needed training too (as we had identified halfway through the lesson). We therefore planned that in the next lesson we would ask them to work out an answer with partners before offering it to the whole class. We hoped this strategy would encourage them to expand on their initial thoughts. I'm glad to say it worked a treat and I now use it to start most lessons.

So although observation itself is not a new concept, the discussion after the lesson was a radical change. In the traditional approach, the teacher is made to feel at fault. By contrast, in the partnership approach, the teacher retains the feeling of being a competent professional. The atmosphere of trust and respect proves motivational because a meaningful two-way exchange sparks further encouragement.

We used the notes from our discussion to help plan another six lessons in the series. As each session went on, I felt more and more comfortable with David's presence in the room. We began to have mini-debriefs through the lesson: 'Try asking that group what they think about such and such…' 'I'm going to spend slightly longer on the next task and add this into the discussion…'

Strategies for developing thinking skills became part of my teaching and the more I used them the more comfortable I became and the more pleased with the results. I could see small changes in the children's attitudes to lessons and, unexpectedly, I could feel a change in my own attitude too.

Then, just as I began to feel comfortable and slightly cocky about my own progress, Dave suggested I should see my own lessons. Puzzled as to how, the penny suddenly dropped: '*Not a video! Never!*'

It took much coaxing and soothing before he finally got a video recorder through the door of my classroom. Having been completely against the idea for my entire career, it is all credit to David and the N-RAIS philosophy that I went along with it. I had complete trust in him.

The curse of the video recorder

So, the dreaded machine arrived and was sited at the back of the room. The lesson began with an attack of stage fright and I became nervy and awkward. My questions and instructions seemed clumsy and everything was just a little embarrassing.

At the end of the lesson, David suggested that I take the video home, so I could get used to seeing myself teach for the first time. The camera sat on the kitchen bench for a long while but I finally took it to the study, closed the door, drew the curtains and pressed 'play'. I spent most of the next 20 minutes looking at my profile in horror, trying desperately to work out where I had got that accent from. Eventually, I managed to watch the video without flinching.

Back in school, David, cleverly and with some sensitivity (again, part of what has made the N-RAIS team a pleasure to work with), never asked to see the tape. Instead, he asked what I thought of seeing myself on video and called that tape 'the practice run.' When I walked into the next lesson, the video camera was set up and, as far as I knew, recording. But I was more in control this time. I knew what I looked and sounded like on video and I knew what to expect when I played it back. This one would show the real me in a real lesson. And it did.

After the lesson, we held a debrief as usual but this time we watched the video at the same time and so I felt much more informed and could see first-hand how the children were responding to discussion and paired work. It is amazing what you miss when you're actually teaching! The video is a useful way of gaining an objective view of the lesson's progress. We continued to use the video for the remaining lessons and I would now happily recommend its use to anyone wishing to improve their teaching.

Principles of effective encouragement

Show faith in each person's basic abilities. Show faith in people as they are, not in how they could be.

Recognise and focus on strengths and assets.

Help people to define and achieve goals.

Use people's interests and aspirations to energise their development.

Be aware of people's feelings and the meanings they make out of their experiences. Ask questions, listen and try to understand.

Model the re-framing of problems and pessimistic thinking to energise effort.

Engineer opportunities for successful achievement.

Be pleased with efforts and contributions.

Promote the idea that it is good to try – failure is no crime and is the inevitable prerequisite of eventual success.

These principles, taken from Chapter 3 (p. 76), are appropriate for supporting teachers as well as learners.

Pupil progress and changes in the classroom

Following the N-RAIS intervention, I have noticed a general improvement in the children's attitudes to work (although 'attitude' is difficult to measure). Where once they would enter the classroom and say, 'We're not doing that, are we?' they now ask, 'Can we do another lesson like the one we did yesterday?' – a small indication of their changing perceptions. Half the battle with classroom management is having enthusiastic children who enjoy their lessons. If they enter the classroom willing to work, then good behaviour is easier to maintain.

My pupils seemed more attentive. They responded more carefully to each other and could talk more clearly about their own learning. I believe that these changes were the result of giving them more demanding tasks and having higher expectations of what they could achieve. Pupils are now expected to give longer answers and have discussions to explore their understanding and justify their opinions.

Pupil contributions of 15 seconds or more are not uncommon in discussions. The average response to a teacher's question is under two seconds. In order to make discussions more effective, we have developed a set of rules for talk. These were negotiated with pupils and are now displayed on anchor charts on the classroom wall. They remind children to respond, for example, to what other pupils *say* without criticising them as *people*. Ground rules reinforce a positive atmosphere of respect in the classroom.

I firmly believe that the teacher's enthusiasm for learning will have a direct impact on the pupils' enthusiasm. When the teacher enjoys the lesson, demonstrates expertise and skill in managing it and sets appropriate challenges, the children respond very positively.

The debrief is now a fundamental part of every lesson. I would rather cut short the main task in order to have the debrief than exclude the debrief to finish the task. It is in the debrief that I have noticed most changes because that is when the pupils discuss their understanding, their attitudes and, most importantly, their learning.

It is no coincidence that my own attitudes and skills in the classroom have improved too. I have learnt a great deal through the encouragement and support I have received and yet feel personal satisfaction in my hard work and effort. Due to the nature of 'thinking' lessons, my own question-and-response skills are gradually becoming more focused. Although this is still developing, I am enjoying the intellectual challenges of orchestrating lessons as much as the pupils are enjoying the challenges of using the N-RAIS strategies.

Continuing the coaching cycle

Teaching is a difficult and unpredictable profession, even more so when you have begun to alter your classroom ethos. It is therefore necessary to put consistent effort into continuing the work that began under supervision. To this end, contact with N-RAIS staff has been regular, though more informal than previously. This encourages me not to revert back to more comfortable – and with hindsight, less productive – practice.

I have also begun to communicate what I have learnt to others, beginning with my own department. Again, this is an opt-in arrangement rather than a departmental or school initiative. Teachers need encouragement too and, with the support of N-RAIS, we are now developing our own coaching programme for teachers. With the right kind of encouragement, perhaps more teachers will opt to reflect on their own practice. I hope so, for I have seen that a school of learning pupils requires a school of learning teachers.

6

Radical Encouragement in Practice

In this chapter, we reflect on the ways that the N-RAIS strategies for Radical Encouragement have been used in Northumberland schools. We argue that the strategies complement each other and have potential for combining together in a coherent programme of school development.

WE HAVE DEFINED Radical Encouragement as 'the deliberate application of multiple strategies by an organisation to encourage the dispositions, strategies and skills necessary for persistent and positive self-development by people within its sphere of influence.' The strategies most often promoted by N-RAIS to achieve these aims in schools were *Philosophy for Children*, teaching thinking skills and coaching. We have seen that staff in schools chose the strategies *they* wanted to adopt. They were not forced to commit themselves to a large-scale programme of school development. At the same time, some of the most interesting projects, such as work with the schools councils at Horton Grange First School and Tyndale Middle School, combined the strategies to good effect. We can analyse how the strategies complemented each other in order to draw out some general principles.

Encouragement and trust

When Carol Oliver, head of Horton Grange First School, set up the school council, she trusted the children to make good judgements. This principle of encouragement is important.[49] Teachers must show faith that learners will rise to the challenges they are set. The culture of the school had to enable children to take time to talk before making decisions, develop their values and take risks. Carol also knew that her children needed help and guidance. Setting up a school council is not the only way that schools can show faith in pupils, challenge them and build a culture for learning. The following ideas could have a similar effect:

- Working with outside partners, such as artists, scientists and businesses, on projects to challenge pupils.
- Consulting pupils on their experiences of learning in the school.[50]
- Encouraging pupils to research issues in the school and the community.[51]
- Giving pupils more opportunities to follow their own interests.
- Devising an imaginative programme of assemblies to promote the sorts of positive learning dispositions outlined in Chapter 1.
- Giving pupils more responsibility for the day-to-day running of aspects of school life such as assemblies, clubs, displays, events and projects in the community.[52]
- Challenging pupils to help each other achieve the best possible grades in exams. This would involve working with pupils to devise plans and evaluations.

The principles that underpin all these ideas are the same: consult pupils, set up challenging projects with them and trust that they can rise to the challenges. At the same time, teachers must recognise that pupils will need support and that the culture of the school, including the peer cultures of pupils, will be one of the most important factors for success.

The philosophical dimension

When schools introduce philosophical enquiry, as Horton Grange and Tyndale did, they create a forum for pupils to question, discuss values and develop thinking skills through dialogue. Pupils come to see themselves as people who are capable of thinking and contributing to the intellectual wellbeing of their group. The community of enquiry, with its emphasis on listening, respect for others and intellectual adventure, is also the ideal environment in which to nurture dispositions such as care, curiosity, collaboration, imagination and reflectivity. Philosophical enquiry supports pupils in meeting challenges in several ways:

- It develops pupils' skills in thinking, listening and working together.
- It prepares them for situations in which they must make judgements about a significant and complex issue.
- It develops positive dispositions for learning.
- It encourages pupils to adopt a 'story' about themselves as capable thinkers.
- It provides a forum where questions about values, cultures and attitudes can be raised and discussed.

This last point is important and deserves some elaboration. Teachers in every school will want to promote a culture that values positive dispositions, achievements, talents and moral behaviour. They will want to influence pupils' perceptions in much the same way as advertisers do when persuading consumers to buy a product. They will state their values, point to good models, draw attention to positive behaviours and reward them. Yet when the prevailing pupil culture in a school does not align with positive values for learning, campaigns for better ways of thinking may not have as much impact as teachers would like. The advantage of philosophical enquiry is that it provides a forum for dialogue. In a community of enquiry, communication runs both ways and so indoctrination (justified as it is) is balanced by argument and reflection. Having a dialogue has a much deeper impact on people than being lectured at, particularly when others listen and respond.

At Tyndale Middle School, council representatives were coached to lead classroom communities of enquiry. The idea of empowering pupils in this way has been tried in other schools across the country. It has obvious benefits for the pupils involved but it also energises the intellectual life of the whole school. Discussions become less dependent on the teacher and self-regulating clubs can emerge. In Berwick, some pupils became so experienced and confident that they could hold their own with local politicians, teachers and school managers in meetings organised to debate school issues. These children were good models for their peers because their thoughtfulness gained the respect of adults.

Philosophical enquiry is not only suitable for primary and middle schools but for secondary schools too. There is scope for philosophy in *Personal, Social and Health Education* and in *Citizenship*. Most subjects also have a philosophical dimension that could be enhanced through a classroom community of enquiry. Some secondary schools have found that philosophy clubs can have a powerful impact on school culture. Teachers at Kingsbrook School in Northamptonshire started a *Philosophy Club* project which had remarkable effects. The following passage comes from the project website:[53]

> *Philosophy for Children* (P4C) began as a pilot scheme in 2000 for a cohort of students in Year 9 we called 'The Lost Children'. The students were reasonably able but were quiet and content to take a 'back seat' during lessons. We felt that by targeting these students we could make a transformational difference to their learning-power and confidence.
>
> We now have a weekly mixed-age P4C Club totally run and facilitated by the students themselves – and with Lost Children cohorts in each year group. A team of trained P4C teachers maintain the regular off-timetable slot, and manage PSE lessons and tutorials using the P4C approach.
>
> P4C is also embedded across the curriculum in several subject areas. We have a strong 'student voice' at Kingsbrook, where confidence, self-esteem and mutual respect are dominant features and students are involved at all levels of school improvement, influenced greatly by P4C. Many Year 11 students made the most of the opportunities that P4C offered in 2005. The club regularly attracted between 20-30 students, with a majority of boys – over half of them from Year 11. Several have testified to the empowering effect that P4C has had in helping them to achieve some excellent individual performances.

Thinking skills and philosophy work together

Philosophical enquiry develops thinking skills because it provides a forum wherein pupils can make moves that are important for dialogue and thinking. These include:

- connecting reasons and conclusions
- seeking examples of and counter-examples to principles
- playing devil's advocate
- using connecting concepts such as *same, different, cause and effect* to make meanings

The teacher can introduce, model and support these moves during the dialogue. However, pupils may need extra support to understand concepts like *cause and effect*. The use of visual tools and focused tasks that we associate with the teaching of thinking skills are useful for clarifying concepts and showing how they are used. So philosophical enquiry and teaching thinking skills support each other. Enquiry gives a forum for the use of skills and the skills enable pupils to cope with the conceptual demands of the enquiry. This is true even if a community of enquiry is scientific or historical rather than philosophical. Matthew Lipman, founder of *Philosophy for Children,* stresses the importance of conceptual 'exercises' to develop conceptual understanding and facility with reasoning moves because he recognises the importance of dialogue and skills developing together.

We have seen that debriefing and 'thinking about thinking' are important for the transfer of thinking skills to new subject areas. When classes are familiar with the community of enquiry, they will be practised in the kinds of dialogue skills required for effective debriefing. They will be able to listen carefully to others and be confident in offering their ideas for discussion. Philosophical enquiry and instruction in thinking skills will, together, offer a culture of intellectual encouragement. George Myerson, in discussing the conditions for intellectual encouragement in education and society, offers some suggestions based on his wide experience of studying dialogue:[54]

The following are conditions of intellectual encouragement:

1. people being disposed to communicate ideas, and therefore contexts in which it is safe and easy to do so;

2. ways of thinking which favour comparisons, which are relative in that sense, not necessarily relativistic;

3. creative forms of negation, which present new possibilities, or which supplement previous propositions;

4. active tolerance of difficult emotions involved in the exchange of ideas and opinions.

The following are conditions of intellectual discouragement:

1. social unfairness, prejudicial stereotypes, threat and menace to identity;

2. the keeping of ideas in storage, intellectual stockpiling;

3. premature refutations, the assumption that it is necessary to negate ideas immediately, without seeing where they lead;

4. a single model of argument or conduct in argument.

Having both philosophy and the teaching of thinking skills in the curriculum together could fulfil Myerson's conditions for intellectual encouragement and help avoid the conditions for discouragement. For example, the community of enquiry provides a safe environment for communicating ideas while Edward de Bono's *CAF* and *Six Thinking Hats* strategies help teachers and learners avoid the trap of 'premature refutation'.

Coaching, philosophy and thinking skills

In Chapter 3, we saw how coaching, philosophy and thinking skills could work together productively. The essential components of coaching are the setting of goals, encouragement, modelling, feeding forward and feeding back. Coaching techniques are suitable for groups and individuals, students and teachers. But an important point to remember is that the term *coaching* is borrowed from a sporting context where the involvement with the coach is voluntary and the client already has an enthusiasm for the sport. In education, teachers and learners are not often united in common goals of learning. For this reason, dialogue about the appropriateness of coaching goals and the underlying values of the coaching initiative will be particularly important. Once again, the community of enquiry can provide a vehicle for such dialogue. Perhaps the greatest contribution coaching can make in education is that it will offer teachers some imaginative ideas for setting up cycles of feeding forward and feeding back which are so important for successful learning. After analysing thousands of research studies, Professor John Hattie of Auckland University identified feedback as the most powerful single factor that enhances achievement in schools.[55]

Familiarity with coaching techniques such as anchor charts and encouragement circles[56] will enable teachers to ensure that feedback is experienced by pupils in ways that are enjoyable and effective.

Developing positive relationships

Professor Andy Hargreaves[57] has argued that 'our change efforts have been so preoccupied with skills and standards that they have not gotten to the heart of what a great deal of teaching is about: establishing bonds and forming relationships with students, making classrooms into places of excitement and wonder, ensuring that all students are included and that no-one feels an outcast.' The strategies promoted by the N-RAIS team will assist teachers in forming positive relationships with learners because they are rooted in encouragement and dialogue. They provide opportunities for teachers to listen to pupils and also offer them effective support without which progress and, therefore, continued co-operation would be less likely.

Daily routines

Philosophy for Children, teaching thinking skills and coaching are three major strategies for Radical Encouragement. This does not mean, however, that daily routines are not important. The strategies will flourish best in schools where dialogue is part of the normal life of a school and where routines support the development of dispositions. For example, school staff who want to foster curiosity will create plenty of opportunities for pupils to devise questions and enquire into the answers.

STEPS towards creating a community of learning

We now offer an outline of the steps a school might take towards Radical Encouragement. The precise order is optional.

DISPOSITIONS. Discuss what dispositions you want learners to develop in your school. Agree a list of key dispositions. Decide how staff in all curriculum areas and key stages will contribute to developing the dispositions you choose. How will they monitor their efforts?

CULTURES. Assess the cultures in your school (including peer cultures). Do the cultures support the dispositions you wish to develop? If, not discuss how you will try to interact with existing cultures so they are more supportive of the dispositions. Decide on whole-school initiatives to promote positive cultures and attitudes.

LISTEN TO LEARNERS. How do you consult students about their learning and their feelings about school? How can you integrate dialogue with learners into lessons and beyond?[58]

PHILOSOPHY. Introduce philosophical enquiry. Encourage those teachers who see the benefits of philosophical enquiry with learners.[59] Create opportunities for teachers and learners to philosophise together. Set up a philosophy research group.

THINKING SKILLS. Try teaching thinking skills in all subjects but remember that they will not transfer without dialogue, thinking about thinking and debriefing. Aim for students to understand important concepts for making meaning. Set up a thinking skills research group.

COACHING. Encourage staff to study techniques of coaching to widen their repertoire of ways to challenge students, encourage them and enable feedback. Encourage teachers to coach each other and to set up circles of encouragement[60] in which teachers can help each other set goals for their teaching, evaluate and make adjustments.

INDEPENDENCE. Do not accept programmes and advice unthinkingly. Develop your own ideas and priorities. Put your plans to the test and adjust them according to results.

ENCOURAGEMENT. Discuss how well teachers and learners are encouraged in your school. What is most of the encouragement focused on? Discuss how you can encourage learners to develop the key dispositions you have identified.

Notes

Chapter 1: Radical Encouragement explained

1. Perkins, D., Jay, E., and Tishman, S., *Beyond Abilities: A Dispositional Theory of Thinking,* Merrill-Palmer Quarterly, 39 (1) pp. 1–21, January 1993.

2. Perkins, Jay and Tishman. Op. cit.

3. Costa, A. and Kallick, B., *Assessing and Reporting on Habits of Mind,* Alexandria, Virginia, USA: ASCD, 2000.

4. Claxton, G., *Building Learning Power: Helping Young People to Become Good Learners,* TLO, 2000.

5. Hobson, P., *The Cradle of Thought,* London: MacMillan, 2002.

6. Richards, I. A., *The Secret of Feedforward,* Saturday Review, pp. 14-17 (3 Feb. 1968). Reprinted in: Richards, I. A., *Complementarities,* Cambridge: Harvard University Press, 1976. See also essays by Richards in Ann E. Berthoff, *Richards on Rhetoric,* Oxford University Press, 1991.

7. Dreikurs, R., *The Challenge of Child Training: A Parents' Guide,* New York: Hawthorn Books, 1972.

8. Dreikurs, R. and Dinkmeyer, D., *Encouraging Children to Learn,* Brunner Routledge, 2000.

9.   Sharron, H. and Coulter, M., *Changing Children's Minds: Feuerstein's Revolution in the Teaching of Intelligence*, Birmingham: Imaginative Minds, 1994.

10. Sharron, H. and Coulter, M., Op. cit.

11. See Lipman, M., *Philosophy Goes to School*, Philadelphia: Temple University Press, 1988.

Chapter 2: Philosophy for Children

12. See: *www.keele.ac.uk/depts/ed/research/cfss-survey-users.htm*

13. The explanation of PC4 in this section is taken from the 'What is P4C?' section of the SAPERE website: *www.sapere.org.uk*. SAPERE (Society for the Advancement of Philosophical Enquiry and Reflection in Education) is a British organisation that co-ordinates philosophical enquiry with children. A reading list of writing in this field by British authors is also available on the website.

14. Splitter, L., 'On the theme of Teaching for Higher Order Thinking Skills' in *Inquiry: Critical Thinking Across the Disciplines*, Montclair State University, Vol. XIV, No. 4. 1995. See also Splitter, Laurance and Sharp, Ann M., *Teaching for Better Thinking: The Classroom Community of Inquiry,* Melbourne, Australia: The Australian Council for Educational Research Ltd, 1995.

15. Courses for teachers are provided nationally by SAPERE. Details are available on the SAPERE website: *www.sapere.org.uk*

16. SAPERE website, Op. Cit.

17. Lipman, M., *Thinking in Education,* 2nd Edition, Cambridge, UK: Cambridge University Press, 2003.

18. Splitter, L., Op. cit.

19. Splitter, L., Op. cit.

20. Resnick, L., *Education and Learning to Think*, Washington, DC: National Academy Press, 1987.

21. Bloom, B. S., *Taxonomy of Educational Objectives, Handbook I: The Cognitive Domain,* New York: David McKay Co Inc., 1956.

22. Trickey, S. and Topping, K. J., *'Philosophy for Children': A Systematic Review,* Research Papers in Education, 2004.

23. *Times Educational Supplement,* 19 September 2003

24. Vygotsky, L., *Thought and Language,* Cambridge, MA: MIT Press, 1986.

25. Claxton, G., *Wise-Up: The Challenge of Lifelong Learning,* London: Bloomsbury, 1999.

26. Hobson, P., Op. cit.

Chapter 3: Coaching

27. Dreikurs, R., Op. cit.

28. School staff can also opt for a certificated course in *Outsmart*. This programme is supported in North Northumberland through the Schools Sports Coordinators' Initiative which now provides funding to enable school staff to implement an *Outsmart* programme in their school. They also have the opportunity to become a coach in order that *Outsmart* becomes a self-propagating training system developed by school staff and supported by N-RAIS. Successful completion of the course gains staff a series of resources designed to help them organise *Outsmart* in their own schools.

29. Dreikurs, R. and Dinkmeyer, D., Op. cit., p. 50. See also Dinkmeyer, D. and Losconcy, L., *The Skills of Encouragement: Bringing Out the Best in Yourself and Others,* St. Lucie Press, 1996. Dinkmeyer, D. and Eckstein, D., *Leadership by Encouragement,* St. Lucie Press, 1996.

Chapter 4: Teaching thinking skills

30. See Caviglioli, O., Harris, I. and Tindall, B., *Thinking Skills and Eye Q*, Network Educational Press, 2002.

31. de Bono, E., *Teach Your Child How to Think,* Penguin, 1994.

32. Wegerif, R., *Thinking Skills, Technology and Learning: A Review of the Literature,* for NESTA FutureLab (*www.nestafuturelab.org*), 50 pages, 2002.

33. See Marzano, R. J., *A Theory-based Meta-Analysis of Research on Instruction*, Aurora, Colorado, Mid-continent Regional Educational Laboratory, p. 170, 1998.

34. Summarised in Wegerif, R., Op. cit.

35. Richards, I. A., Op. cit., 1976.

36. For example: Wallace, B., Maker, J., Cave, D. and Chandler, S., *Thinking Skills and Problem-solving – an Inclusive Approach: A Practical Guide for Teachers in Primary Schools*, NACE/Fulton Publication, 2004. Also the 'debriefing' referred to in Leat, D., *Thinking Through Geography*, 2nd Edition, Cambridge: Chris Kington, 2002.

37. DfES, *Key Stage 3 National Strategy Key Messages about Teaching Thinking*, 2003. This document can be found at: *www.standards.dfes.gov.uk/keystage3*

38. DfES, Op. cit.

39. Richards, I. A., *How to Read a Page: A Course in Effective Reading, with an Introduction to a Hundred Great Words*, Routledge, 1943.

40. Vygotsky, L., Op. cit., (Chapter on the Development of Scientific Concepts in Childhood)

41. See Buzan, T., *Use Your Head*, BBC Books, 1995. See also Caviglioli, O., Harris, I. and Tindall, B., Op. cit.

42. See Higgins, S., *Thinking Through Primary Teaching*, Cambridge, Chris Kington Publishing, 2001.

43. See Leat, D., *Thinking Through Geography*, 2nd Edition, Cambridge: Chris Kington, 2002.

44. See Leat, D., 2002, Op. cit., and Higgins, S., 2001, Op. cit.

45. See Echevarria, A., *On Target for Transfer*, Teaching Thinking and Creativity magazine, Issue 17, 2005.

46. See Leat, D., Op. cit.

47. This example is an elaboration of a passage from: Tharp, R. G. & Gallimore, R., *Rousing Minds to Life: Teaching, Learning & Schooling in Social Context*, Cambridge: Cambridge Universtiy Press, 1989.

48. de Bono, E., Op. cit.

Chapter 6: Radical Encouragement in practice

49. See the principles of encouragement on page 70 of this book.

50. Researchers Jean Ruddock and Julia Flutter argue convincingly that consultation with pupils in and out of lessons is one of the most powerful strategies for school improvement. See: Ruddock, J. and Flutter, J., *How to Improve Your School,* Continuum, 2004.

51. Kellett, M., *How to Develop Children as Researchers: A Step-by-Step Guide to Teaching the Research Process,* London: Paul Chapman Publishing, 2005.

52. See Jason Cauchi's innovative scheme in Cauchi, J., *Serve to Lead*, Teaching Thinking and Creativity magazine, Issue 16, 2005.

53. See the Kingsbrook philosophy project website at: *www.p4ckingsbrook.org*

54. Myerson, G., *Rhetoric, Reason and Society*, Sage Publications, p. 151, 1994.

55. Hattie, J., *Inaugural Lecture: Professor of Education*, University of Auckland, 1999.

56. For encouragement circles, see Dinkmeyer, D. and Eckstein, D., *Leadership by Encouragement,* St. Lucie Press, 1996.

57. Hargreaves, A., *Rethinking Educational Change with Heart and Mind*, ASCD Yearbook, 1997.

58. See Ruddock, J. and Flutter J., Op. cit.

59. We recommend that teachers who can see the benefits of philosophical enquiry attend a course before they try it out. See SAPERE website: *www.sapere.org.uk*

60. Dinkmeyer, D. and Eckstein, D., Op. cit., 1996.

Appendix 1

The N-RAIS team

David Kinninment is a former teacher of geography and head of a large humanities faculty. He taught for 11 years before joining N-RAIS in May 2003. He has contributed to geography text books and been involved in the development of teaching thinking, initially through geography, working with Newcastle University since the early 1990s. He co-edited *More thinking through Geography,* published by Chris Kington, and contributed to other books in the 'thinking through' series. He conducted research into teaching thinking and assessment for learning. His former department was successful, he believes, because it looked beyond the subject to underlying transferable concepts and skills.

James Nottingham. Before co-founding the RAIS project, James Nottingham had been, at various stages, a class teacher, a head of department, a childcare officer, a charity worker and a pig farmer. He has worked with children of all ages and was instrumental in developing a network of *Philosophy for Children* practitioners across north-east England. As well as being one of the directors of N-RAIS, James is now a sought-after keynote speaker on thinking skills, *Philosophy for Children* and Radical Encouragement. He writes for *Teaching Thinking and Creativity* magazine and for the Scholastic publications, *Child Education* and *Junior Education*. He is also the UK director of *Teacher Designed Schools*, an international network that encourages teachers to devise a shared vision of what their school might be.

Ian Patience. Long-standing interests in education and art have led Ian to work as a professional stained glass window-maker, a community educator for the Open University, a mosaicist, a teacher of middle school children, an artist with work in private and public collections, a consultant for Northumberland's Thinking for Learning Unit and, currently, a consultant for N-RAIS. Recent projects with Creative Partnerships and the University of Northumbria (in collaboration with the Baltic Centre for Contemporary Art) have continued his research into the nature, value and cultivation of creativity. Ian's enquiry-based approach involves him in working alongside teachers, parents and children in shared investigations into learning and teaching that are rooted in the values of pragmatist philosophy. He has written for both art and educational journals and has co-developed courses and resources.

Jill Nottingham has developed courses to encourage and challenge the thinking of pre-school and primary-age children. She has designed resources to stimulate critical and creative thinking with these age groups. Jill is an accredited SAPERE *Philosophy for Children* trainer and has delivered many successful P4C and thinking-skills courses in the UK and internationally. She believes strongly in the importance of the role of family and community in developing successful pupil learning and she has co-written course and accompanying materials to aid parents and carers in supporting children's learning outside schools. Jill has taught all the key stages.

Michael Henry is a former headteacher of a successful 9–13 middle school. He was appointed director of the N-RAIS project in September 2000 and led its development into a team of nine consultants working with five communities, including almost 100 schools. In addition to being an accredited SAPERE *Philosophy for Children* and *Investment in*

Excellence trainer, he is a key facilitator for the National College of School Leadership, working on the highly-acclaimed *New Vision* programme supporting newly-appointed headteachers.

Louise Brown is passionate about encouraging thinking in young children through her work with schools, parents and community groups. She is committed to developing and facilitating courses such as *Philosophy for Children*, *Developing Babies' Brains* and *Teaching Thinking* to a range of audiences. Louise has considerable experience of teaching all the key stages.

Paul Dearlove has in the past been an officer in the Merchant Navy, an industrial training officer, teacher, deputy head and principal of an outdoor school in Denmark. He brings an interesting blend into his work from a variety of education and training backgrounds and from his other main interest as a coach. Paul is a life coach, Neuro-Linguistic Programming (NLP) practitioner, and a *Philosophy for Children* trainer.

Joanne Bush has experienced great success in using teaching thinking strategies, *Philosophy for Children* and encouraging self-belief in young people from the early years through to the sixth form. She has a strong commitment to enabling young women to realise their potential and to develop their self-worth. As a result of this she has developed the successful *Girls Realising Their Own Worth* (GROW) course.

Katherine Vero is particularly interested in working with young children and their families. She has developed courses that include *Developing Babies' Brains* and *Philosophical Skills for the Young*. Katherine is an NLP practitioner and is currently participating in the Anthony Robbins Mastery University. Katherine is an experienced teacher of early years children.

Appendix 2

N-RAIS contacts and courses

N-RAIS contact details

N-RAIS Project   Tel: +44 (0) 1289 332816
The Community Centre   Fax: +44 (0) 1289 332816
Palace Street East
Berwick-upon-Tweed   **Website**: www.rais.org.uk
Northumberland
TD15 1HT
United Kingdom

N-RAIS COURSES and initiatives that put the principles of Radical Encouragement into practice have been referred to throughout the book. For example:

- Philosophy for Children (Chapter 2)
- Outsmart (Chapter 3)
- Support your child's learning (Chapter 3)
- Encouraging self-belief (Chapter 3)
- Teaching thinking skills (Chapter 4)
- N-RAIS days and staff support (Chapter 5)

A full list of N-RAIS courses is available on its website: *www.rais.org.uk.* Other courses are summarised on the next page.

GROW: Girls Realising Their Own Worth

GROW is a 12-hour course designed to empower girls and young women to realise their own worth. The course aims to raise the aspirations of young women who have low self-esteem.

GROW was designed in response to work with young people and to what is also becoming recognised as a national problem, the alarmingly increasing rate of low self-esteem and low aspirations in girls and young women.

Over the past three years, N–RAIS has worked with parents, teachers, school nurses, Northumberland's Teenage Pregnancy Unit and youth workers, all of whom have raised their concerns at the self-critical and negative behaviours, beliefs and attitudes which many girls, young women and young mothers display.

The GROW programme works with girls and young women aged 12-18. The groups are generally kept to fewer than 10 participants as one of the key aims is to establish a caring, trusting and mutually supportive community of young women. Either school staff will nominate participants or the girls themselves will decide who should attend the course. The programme is for any young woman who displays beliefs, attitudes or behaviours which would suggest that they have low aspirations and self-esteem. The girls usually fall into one of the following categories:

a. Girls who are very shy and unsure of themselves – the type of person who normally 'disappears' in the classroom.
b. Girls who are vocal in lessons, appear to be confident, often misbehave in the classroom and seek or create attention for themselves.
c. Girls who consistently follow the crowd and are overtly influenced by the beliefs, behaviours and attitudes of others.
d. Girls who display high levels of academic ability but who may not be achieving their full potential because of a lack of self-esteem.
e. Girls who have a poor image of themselves.

The course is delivered using a variety of strategies and approaches which are at the heart of Radical Encouragement, such as coaching and philosophical enquiry

A number of girls who have attended this course are now more positive about themselves. A consistently positive factor was the difference that being part of a mutually supportive community made to their contributions and confidence. Some girls have taken action to make their goals a reality and have realised that they have a responsibility for their future. All the girls expressed their delight in being able to voice their thoughts without being judged or shouted down.

Developing Babies' Brains

The first five years of a child's life are critical for emotional and social development as the infant builds strong bonds with the people who provide consistent care. Babies also have a predisposition to learn language, so it is natural for them to absorb words and sounds and new concepts.

The N-RAIS *Developing Babies' Brains* course is for parents, childcare professionals, health professionals, and anyone who is concerned with the care of the very young. We use Radical Encouragement strategies to support participants in their understanding of the development of behaviour, attachment and the intellect. Those who care for and work with the very young and their families have found that the course supports and develops their work. Participants report that they have gained confidence in their understanding of child development and have enjoyed learning collaboratively.

Hybrid courses

An interesting development of the Radical Encouragement work has arisen from requests for 'hybrid' courses which combine elements of the different strategies promoted by N-RAIS. This seems to have grown for a number of reasons:

a. The trust built up in time through the project's work with clients.
b. The belief in the quality of the project's work.

c. The confidence, gained from previous work with project staff, to ask for something a little different.

d. Building a successful partnership network.

In particular, N-RAIS has had requests for events or courses to foster the positive development and leadership of teams and networks. Clients include:

> Blyth Valley County Council
> ICCQ (Improving Croft and Cowpen Quay)
> Princess Louise and Newsham Schools

Positive Leadership

The last ten years have seen a fundamental change in views on leadership. It is no longer seen as the prerogative of those in positions of power. It is recognised that we all have leadership qualities within us. With this in mind, N-RAIS has developed a course for local schools, businesses and community organisations. Participants in the course develop a range of strategies and principles for leadership.

N-RAIS has also teamed up with Bill Martin, an award-winning Principal of Leadership from the US, to support the development of leadership in the UK.

Bill was a primary school teacher, a deputy in a middle school and a principal of four high schools in America, three of which won coveted blue-ribbon status, awarded to the best 300 schools in the country (out of 36,000 high schools). His most recent school, Monroe High, in inner-city Detroit, was deemed to be failing its 2400 students when Bill took over. Five years later, it was the only working-class school to feature in the top 300.

Appendix 3

External evaluation interim report

The work of the N-RAIS project has been evaluated by teams at the universities of Newcastle and Sunderland. A full and final report will appear on the N-RAIS website in 2006. The following conclusions are taken from the *interim* evaluation report. It is not a complete evaluation of the work of N-RAIS.

Conclusions from quantitative data
- At Key Stage 1, long-term involvement in the RAIS initiative has led to improved maths performance in national tests.
- At Key Stage 1, there appears to be a positive link between the use of *Community of Enquiry* and *Cognitive Mapping* thinking skills interventions and maths performance.
- Overall, the use of philosophy approaches is significantly greater in schools where English performance at Key Stage 2 SATs exceeds predicted levels.
- At Key Stage 3 in the 5 RAIS high schools, 567 pupils achieved 5 or more A–C GCSEs in 2004 compared with 457 predicted (i.e. 24% more than predicted). This represents a significant improvement for the RAIS schools but more than half of that improvement can be accounted for by gains in just one school (Berwick High School), which the RAIS team has supported since 2001. This suggests benefits of long-term involvement in the project.
- In the Berwick cluster of first, middle and high schools there has been a sustained whole-school emphasis on thinking skills interventions (especially *Philosophy for Children*) for 3-4 years now and measurable benefits are becoming apparent.

Conclusions from qualitative data

- RAIS consultants are important mediators of teaching and learning.
- RAIS consultants are operating as models of good practice.
- Training sessions are of high quality.
- Something tangible is happening which is having a positive effect upon significant numbers of teachers in Northumberland and is valued by them.
- Teachers repeatedly report that they 'know' thinking skills interventions (particularly Community of Enquiry) are 'working' but, when pressed, they find it difficult to identify their evidence for making this claim beyond reference to anecdote and the 'feeling' that classroom interactions are getting better. The identification of indicators and evidence of impact will be central to phase two of the evaluation.
- The effectiveness of the consultancy model being used by RAIS in helping teachers to embed interventions in their practice is significant. This is valued and enjoyed by teachers for the way in which consultants share responsibility for improving practice with teachers rather than merely demonstrating the intervention and leaving the teacher alone to grapple with the practicalities of making it happen in the classroom.
- There is some evidence of rising aspirations in pupils and parents.

Interim report by: Dr. Maggie Gregson and Trish Spedding, University of Sunderland, in partnership with David Moseley and Dr. Vivienne Baumfield, University of Newcastle upon Tyne.